POWER AND INVOLVEMENT IN ORGANIZATIONS

To M.G. - missed you.

Power and Involvement in Organizations

An empirical examination of Etzioni's compliance theory

HELGA DRUMMOND

Avebury

Aldershot · Brookfield USA · Hong Kong · Singapore · Sydney

Published by
Avebury
Ashgate Publishing Limited
Gower House
Croft Road
Aldershot
Hants GU11 3HR
England

Ashgate Publishing Company
Old Post Road
Brookfield
Vermont 05036
USA

British Library Cataloguing in Publication Data
Drummond, Helga
Power and Involvement in Organisations:
Empirical Examinations of Etzioni's
Compliance Theory
I. Title
302.3

ISBN 1 85628 474 3

Printed and Bound in Great Britain by
Athenaeum Press Ltd, Newcastle upon Tyne.

Contents

Figures and tables

Acknowledgements

I thank my former Ph. D. supervisors, Chris Allinson and Terry Moreton of Leeds University for their enthusiasm and support. I am also grateful to Helen Bird, Val Fry, Lynda Moore and Nick Walkley of the Institute for their technical assistance. It is an understatement to say that without them, this book would not have been produced.

Introduction

The topic of this research is Etzioni's Compliance Theory (1975). The theory, which is described in detail later in this book is essentially concerned with the different kinds of power used by organizations. It has a place both in the literature on the structure of organizations and also on the motivation of people within them.

Etzioni's treatment of power can be traced to Russell (1938) and to Marx. For Russell and Etzioni, organizations serve as the criterion for the classification of power. Both view power as a structural phenomenon. The organization provides the mechanism through which it is exercised. Power is embodied in role formalization, division of labour a hierarchial structure and so forth.

Russell classifies power over human beings by means of three separate criteria, each criterion in turn produces its own forms of power. The first criterion is the manner of influencing individuals, which may be carried out through physical coercion, material inducements or persuasion. Another criterion of classifying power is by the type of organization involved. The types of power formulated by the previous criterion form the basis of grouping. For example, the army and police are classified as organizations which exercise coercive power. Economic organizations are categorised as using inducement power whilst schools, churches and political parties are grouped together on the basis that they aim to influence opinion and consequently rely on persuasion.

The third criterion is psychological. According to Russell there are three such sources of power. One is tradition based upon respect such as that accorded to spiritual and temporal leaders. When tradition begins to fade, either revolutionary power arises based on new beliefs or, so called naked power emerges based on fear and personal ambition.

It will become apparent that Etzioni's typology of power relies on criteria very similar to the first two described by Russell. Etzioni classifies organizations according to their goals which are order, economic, or value based. This corresponds to reliance upon a particular form of power, coercion, remunerative or symbolic. The difference between Etzioni and Russell is that Etzioni views power as possession of assets. In this sense Etzioni identifies with Marx's view of power as resting on inequality.

Power therefore constitutes the structural aspect of Etzioni's theory. Its motivational element is embodied in what is known as involvement. Involvement is defined as attachment and loyalty to the organization. The concept identifies with the literature on human needs, participative management and organizational identification (Maslow, 1954; Argyris, 1964; Kelman, 1958; Mowday, Porter and Steers 1982). The various theories of involvement are described within the book. Here it is important to note that the difference between other writers and Etzioni, is that Etzioni specifically links involvement to power.

It is clear from an examination of the literature that whereas there are studies of power (e.g., Kipnis, 1972; Kipnis, 1976), and studies of involvement, (e.g., Lawler and Hall, 1970; Buchanan, 1974), there are very few studies of the relationship between power and involvement, and still fewer of power and involvement in the context of Etzioni's theory. Indeed Etzioni's theory is virtually unresearched which is surprising in view of its popularity among students of organization.

A number of reasons can be suggested for this. Although

Russell might argue that power is the fundamental concept in social science and, although Bierstedt (1950, p.784) might claim 'without power there is no organization and without organization there is no order', power generally has been relatively underemphasised in the study of organizations (Pfeffer, 1981). Pfeffer attributes this partly to competing perspectives for understanding behaviour especially those with a more direct relevance to productivity.

Another reason for neglect may be the problematic nature of the concept. As Bierstedt (1950) said, everyone knows what power is until they try to define it. Wrong (1979, p.65) described the field of power theory as 'chaotic'. For instance, 'Power is regarded as influence, or influence as a form of power . . . . Authority is a sub type of power, or power and authority are distinct and opposite. Persuasion is a form of power; it is not a form of power at all. Force is a form of power; it is not power.'

Another possibility is that the study of power in organizations has not captured the imagination in the same way as motivational theories pertaining to involvement and alienation. Etzioni (1968, b) in his book 'The Active Society', writing in the mid 1960's, referred to the 'deep alienation' of people within organizations. The book links compliance theory to peace, to flowers and is imbued with a sense of humanity, hope and despair.

Whatever the realities beneath the rhetoric it is difficult to resist its inspirational appeal. The study of power in organizations has been more prosaic. It has concentrated on identifying the sources of power in organizations. As such it has emphasised the structural aspects of power. One of the earliest contributions in this area was the 'strategic contingencies' theory (Hickson, Hinings, Lee, Schneck and Pennings, 1971). This described power in organizations as emanating from sub units. The theory proposes that the power of a sub-unit is determined by its relationship to other sub-units in the organization, and by its response to the environment. The

3

division of labour creates interdependency between units, imbalances of interdependency result in power relations. The strategic contingencies theory formed the basis of subsequent theoretical contributions which have been concerned with integrating various system perspectives such as network centrality, resources dependency, formal authority, environmental factors and so on (Astley and Sachdeva, 1984; Cobb, 1984; Mintzberg, 1984).

It is only relatively recently that psychological aspects of power in organizations have begun to receive attention in the literature. Whereas twenty years ago, discussions of power in organizations often began and ended with a swift resume of French and Raven's (1968) typology, more recently, writers have begun to include material on personal aspects of power (e.g., McClelland, 1975) and the impact of rewards and punishments (e.g., Arvey and Ivancevich, 1980; Schnake and Dumler, 1989). There is growing recognition that sources of power in organizations go beyond structure to include personality, gender differentiation, symbolism and language to name but a few (Morgan, 1986; Clegg, 1989).

Despite its somewhat arid treatment in the literature, power is by no means a dull subject. It is surrounded by connotations of the supernatural, the invisible world, a spiritual cosmology and the departed dead (Becker, 1975). Perhaps the problem is that power in organizations has been studied in a vacuum. The importance of Etzioni's theory as a research topic stems not only from its simplicity in an area beset by complexity, but because it links power to another variable, involvement.

Involvement focuses upon the process whereby individuals become linked to the organization and how these links become strengthened or broken. As such, Etzioni's concept of involvement bears close resemblance to the concept of organizational commitment. Although organization commitment continues to attract considerable research attention, few studies have examined the relationship between power and

4

commitment. Possibly this is because power tends to be regarded as a sociological phenomenon whereas commitment has tended to be studied by psychologists. The accumulation of evidence suggests that commitment is affected by a combination of personal and situational variables such as age, tenure and satisfaction (Mathieu and Zajac, 1990). Only a handful of studies have examined the impact of psychological constructs of reward and punishment - factors closely allied to power.

Approaching the research

This study is fundamentally concerned with testing the core element of Etzioni's theory, that is the relationship between various types of organization and respective levels of power and involvement. It will become apparent however, that there is more to Etzioni's theory than text book summaries suggest. The relationship between power and involvement forms the touch stone of a whole series of interrelations based on the idea of concomitant variation. Some of these are developed and explored in this research. Etzioni's theory may be conceived of as a set of discrete organizational power and involvement combinations. The research model builds on this and proposes systematic variations in power, involvement, and work alienation across a range of organizations including both archetypal examples of Etzioni's threefold classification of organizations and organizations defined as intermediate types. The research also examines compliance relations within organizations be seeking to establish whether power and involvement vary systematically by organization level.

The approach to the topic has been to take Etzioni's concepts as he defines them and to concentrate upon developing and testing the relationships between them. It is acknowledged that Etzioni's theory is not without weaknesses though it is argued that these need to be addressed by research rather than by discourse alone. In particular, it seemed important to avoid becoming side tracked by the so called 'power debate' though without, it is hoped, side-stepping the relevant theoretical and methodological issues surrounding Etzioni's treatment of the subject. Power and involvement are regarded in this book as equally important though inevitably, the literature on involvement and in particular that on organizational commitment claims a disproportionate amount of space simply because there is so much more work on this subject.

Five organizations participated in the survey. Etzioni's coercive, utilitarian and normative archetypes were represented respectively by a sample of ex-prison inmates, a factory and a voluntary organization. A City Works department of a local government organization and a college stood as examples of intermediate utilitarian and normative organizations respectively.

Symbolic, remunerative and coercive power were measured using items from Sims and Szilalgyi's (1975) Leader Behavior scales with additional items to represent non-contingency coercion, (Podsakoff, Todor, Grover and Huber, 1984). Involvement was measured using items of Cook and Wall's (1981) Organizational Commitment Questionnaire.

The results of the study support Etzioni's basic theory of systematic variations in power and involvement between organizational archetypes. Further, the study shows how the theory can be modified to one which inter-relates not only all three forms of power and involvement but also work alienation - a new correlate. The result is a model which retains all the simplicity of Etzioni's original but enhances its explanatory power.

The study also has implications for the literature concerning leader behaviour and organizational commitment as it indicates the need to incorporate structure into their respective theoretical frameworks.

Structure of the book

Chapter One contains a description of Etzioni's theory and a detailed discussion of his treatment of power. Chapter Two is devoted to an examination of the theory of organizational involvement. Part of the role of this chapter is to differentiate between organizational involvement and related concepts, in particular work alienation. There follows a review of the research. This wide ranging survey is divided into three chapters. Chapter Three concentrates on the sociological literature on so called 'compliance variables' and includes studies of prisons, schools, the church to name but a few. Chapter Four comprises a review of the research into the impact of rewards and punishment on various forms of employee satisfaction plus some studies concerning the use of power in organizations. Chapter Five is devoted to the research into factors affecting organizational commitment.

Chapter Six outlines the research aims and hypotheses. The results of the literature survey are utilised to construct a research model which is a more complex version of Etzioni's original. Its purpose is to facilitate both a testing of the basic theory and to explore the possibility of going beyond it. Chapters Seven and Eight describe the research design and methodology.

The results of the study are outlined in Chapter Nine. The main thrust of the analysis consists of a series of Oneway Analyses of Variance of power, involvement and work alienation between organizations. The key element of this is a comparison between organizations defined as archetypal representatives of Etzioni's taxonomy of organizations. This shows clear evidence of systematic variation on all variables.

Findings are discussed in Chapter Ten. Much of this chapter focuses upon the results pertaining to the wider aspects of the research model where the evidence is more equivocal.

The conclusions of the study are presented in Chapter 11. It is suggested that not only is Etzioni's theory supported in essence, but that it can be modified to improve its explanatory power by extending Etzioni's basic propositions and by the addition of work alienation as a new correlate. The book ends with a discussion of the possibilities for further research.

1 Etzioni's compliance theory

The core compliance theory

This chapter outlines Etzioni's Compliance Theory (Etzioni, 1959, 1965a, 1965b, 1968a, 1975; Etzioni and Lehman, 1980; Gross and Etzioni, 1985). Etzioni begins with a concern to understand why people obey the law and adhere to social norms. He focuses upon organizations because they have goals to attain and that in order to survive they must be effective. Effectiveness requires commitment on the part of organization members. He argues that since this commitment is not usually given voluntarily, organizations must have some mechanism for procuring it. This mechanism involves the application of power. The type of power predominantly used will depend upon the particular goal of the organization.

The vehicle for the application of power is the bureaucratic structure of the organization with its rule frameworks, job description, job specifications and the delegation of authority and responsibilities.

Power, therefore, plays a central role within Etzioni's theory. He defines power as 'An actor's ability to induce or influence another actor to carry out his directives or any other norm he supports' (Etzioni, 1975, p.4).

The three kinds of power identified by Etzioni are coercive, remunerative and symbolic. Coercive power involves the possibility of physical force or sanctions. Remunerative power relates to material rewards, commonly wages and salaries whilst symbolic power entails the use of titles, accolades, social approbation and the like as satisfiers of status and/or ego needs of participants.

The argument is that each of these three types of power engenders particular kinds of involvement in the organization by participants and concomitantly different levels of commitment. Involvement therefore too plays a major role within Etzioni's Compliance Theory. It is defined as 'The cathectic-evaluative orientation of an actor to an object, characterised in terms of intensity and direction' (Etzioni, 1975, p.8). Respectively the three kinds of involvement associated with coercive, remunerative and symbolic power are thought to be alienative and hostile, calculative and mildly positive, and moral and extremely positive. The combination of power and involvement is known as the compliance structure of the organization.

Etzioni's theory is mainly concerned with control of what he calls 'lower participants,' that is, members who are lowest in the organizational hierarchy. In a factory therefore, the theory would be primarily concerned with the control, and the involvement of, shop floor workers.

His argument is that the lower participants are more difficult to control because the rewards on offer are smaller and the impact of their withdrawal is correspondingly less. Three criteria are listed for membership of this group termed 'lower participant'. These are:

1 Their involvement in the organization.

2 The degree of subordination to which they are subjected.

3 The extent to which performance criteria are attached to their roles.

Any organization member scoring highly on one of these falls into the category of 'lower participant' and it is with this category that this research is primarily concerned.

A taxonomy of organizations

Etzioni classifies organizations into three types, namely, coercive, utilitarian and normative according to the predominant form of power used to control lower participants. Coercive organizations are instanced by prisons of one kind or another. Utilitarian organizations are typified by factories whose goals are fundamentally material. Normative organizations are dedicated to the pursuit of non material and sometimes idealistic goals. Examples include, colleges, hospitals and organizations where participants work voluntarily.

Coercive organizations

Etzioni defines coercive organizations as those in which no inmate would voluntarily remain. The major task of such organizations is the forced detention of lower participants involving reliance upon coercion as the means of control.
Coercion is defined as, 'The application, or threat of application, of physical sanctions such as infliction of pain, deformity or death; generation of frustration through restriction of movement or controlling through force the satisfaction of needs such as those for food, sex, comfort and the like,'(Etzioni, 1975, p.5).

Other methods of control it is argued are also coercive. A prisoner performing a service for a guard in return for a cigarette is responding to coercion and not remunerative control. This is because although the reward is material, 'The special value of the cigarette . . . is derived from the segregation of the inmate from regular markets. This segregation is, . . . based on force (Etzioni, 1975, p.27).

11

Coercive organizations may be ranked according to the level of repression. This may be measured as the normal punishment for an offence. Escape from an ordinary prison usually results in loss of remission, escape from a concentration camp is punishable by death. Inmates who arrive in coercive organizations are already hostile as a result of their pre-incarceration experiences. This intensifies in accordance with the amount of coercion then applied.

Utilitarian organizations

The role of utilitarian organizations is the production of goods and services for sale in the market place. Control is necessary to ensure conformity to standards regarding the level and quality of work and to check tardiness, absenteeism and so on. Since they can neither obtain this through force, nor by the intrinsic appeal of their objectives, utilitarian organizations need to purchase it. Remunerative control typically includes wages, salaries, fringe benefits, promotion and training.

Such control results in a calculative attitude towards the organization. Involvement tends to be neither extremely hostile nor extremely committed but is based upon exchange of rewards for commitment. These statements also apply to a lesser degree to blue collar sub-divisions of predominantly normative organizations, for example cleaning and maintenance departments of a university, hospital portering services and so on. In certain organizations such as banking and insurance, lower participants will be white collar employees.

Normative organizations

Very little control is needed by a normative organization. Members tend to arrive with highly positive attitudes reflecting their internalised acceptance of, and commitment to, its goals. Etzioni argues that coercion destroys involvement, and material incentives are inconsistent with an appeal to values.

Normative organizations therefore rely upon the manipulation of symbols, typically praise, recognition, badges and medals. Coercion is rare, if used it tends to be symbolic also, for example, subtle threats and innuendo, excommunication or other ritualised punishment may be used. Certain normative organizations such as schools, mental hospitals and some extreme political and extreme religious sects utilise coercion as a secondary means of control.

Dual organizations and incongruent organizations

To complete the list of organizational types, it is necessary to mention two other categories to which Etzioni refers. The term 'dual organization' is applied to organizations utilising two forms of power simultaneously and equally. These are seen as being different from those which have one predominant power application with secondary reliance upon other types. The military is a dual organization because it relies equally upon symbolic and coercive power. The brave are honoured with medals, cowards are shot. Organizations which apply symbolic power most commonly, and coercive power seldomly, are not dual structures.

The term 'incongruent organizations' is applied to those organizations where the predominant type of power used is inappropriate, in terms of effectiveness, for that organization. For example, praise and recognition in a prison for criminals may be greeted with derision. Similarly material incentives may be wasted if members are already highly committed to the aims of the organization. Etzioni argues that involvement is determined by many other variables besides power, particularly participant's pre organizational experiences. Incongruence may result if these are inconsistent with the organization's compliance structure. Congruency is achieved by modifying the power system or by attempting to regulate involvement through

13

recruitment control, socialization and so on. Figure 1 shows the complete range of possibilities. The cells containing 'x' refer to congruent relationships while those containing 'o' refer to incongruent relationships. It is argued that organizations resist incongruence and simultaneously attempt to realise congruency in order to be effective.

	INVOLVEMENT		
POWER	LOW (ALIENATIVE)	MEDIUM (CALCULATIVE)	HIGH (MORAL)
COERCIVE	X	0	X
REMUNERATIVE	0	X	0
NORMATIVE	0	0	X

Key:

X = congruent power and involvement combinations.

0 = incongruent power and involvement combinations.

Figure 1   Etzioni's power and involvement combinations

accompanying

Concomitant relations: the dominant concept of Etzioni's theory

Etzioni's theory rests on the idea of concomitant relations between power and involvement and other organizational variables. According to Etzioni this means that compliance structures relate systematically to goals, leadership, recruitment, socialization and so on. It is suggested for example, that leadership in normative organizations tends to be expressive, that is avoiding the use of arbitrary authority and not putting unreasonable demands on people, whilst utilitarian organizations tend to adopt a more instrumental approach with stress laid upon production and the maintenance of discipline (Rossel, 1970, 1971). Recruitment likewise tends to be consistent with compliance structures. In coercive organizations recruitment and compliance are by force, in utilitarian organizations by material inducement and in normative ones by symbolic appeal.

Two aspects of the theme of concomitant relations which are important to this research are the idea of a compliance continuum between organizations and the idea of a compliance continuum within them. These are described in more detail below.

A compliance continuum between organizations

It is suggested that within each category of organization, differences of degree exist in the relative emphasis placed upon the predominant mode of control and corresponding level of involvement. Participants in say, an extreme religious sect will experience greater symbolic control than those in a milder example of a normative organization like a college. Inmates of a concentration camp will be more alienated than those of an open prison because of the greater degree of coercion applied in the former.

Systematic differences in power and involvement also occur across the whole range of organizations. It is argued for example that although hospital porters are, 'The most remunerative, least normative group of the hospital staff . . . they are more normatively controlled than blue collar workers in blue collar industries. This fact is reflected in their moral commitment to the health of patients,' (Etzioni, 1975, p.32). What this means is that not only will there be differences in the level of power and involvement between organizations within each of Etzioni's three categories, but there may also be systematic variation between comparable groups of staff across the whole typology of organizations.

A compliance continuum within organizations

Etzioni also suggests that power and involvement might vary by organization level even to the extent of minute differences between echelons. Senior staff in particular, enjoy greater autonomy, greater freedom from coercion, and engage in more absorbing and meaningful work than lower participants. Consequently involvement and satisfaction are higher for senior staff than for lower participants. Systematic differences between organizations may exist at senior levels but these will be less pronounced than those between lower participants because of greater homogeneity of control at senior levels.

Although utilitarian organizations tend to rely upon remuneration to control the lower echelons, differences of degree exist between the various ranks. Control of skilled and semi-skilled blue collar workers, will focus less on remunerative power, and more on symbols than for unskilled staff. The same applies to white collar staff in relation to blue collar workers. Within white collar grades, higher ranking staff such as private secretaries, tend to be more symbolically controlled than lower ranking clerks. Control of semi-professionals is less symbolic than for full professionals. Involvement varies concomitantly.

A critical appraisal of Etzioni's theory

The value of Etzioni's theory is that it enables the recognition of patterns between variables and thus the realities they represent. No model can ever include all the factors impinging upon the situation. Its value depends not on how much it encompasses, but on the subtlety and discernment with which it captures the facets of the situation it represents.

In appraising Etzioni's theory therefore, it is important to be mindful that it is an abstraction which seeks to explain reality simply. The discussion which follows is mainly confined to issues directly concerned with this research and in particular Etzioni's treatment of power.

Classifying organizations

Perrow (1972) has argued that Etzioni does not take into account the wide variations in the climate of management of supposedly similar organizations. Some schools, says Perrow, are run like factories, some factories are run like prisons. Whilst it is difficult to deny Perrow's point, surely the issue is whether, despite all the deviations between supposedly similar organizations, there is a pattern in the relationship between power and involvement. This is a question which can only be answered by research.

Etzioni has suggested that within each category, organizations can be ranked according to the standard punishment for a particular offence. The difficulty with this criterion is that whilst it might be applicable to coercive organizations where attempted escape might attract a range of penalties from execution to loss of remission, it becomes more difficult when applied to employing organizations where dismissal is often the only formal sanction.

It is difficult to see therefore how Etzioni arrives at the classification of various utilitarian and normative organizations. For example, Etzioni does not explain the rationale for classifying professional business organizations as more normative than factories or for regarding colleges and universities as more extreme examples of normative organizations than hospitals (Etzioni, 1968a). Presumably it is on the basis that a factory operative for instance, is more likely to be dismissed than his counterpart in a more normative organization for a specific offence.

Defining the lower participants

Although Etzioni's theory is based upon the so called 'lower participants' it is not clear what is meant by this. The criteria for ascertaining membership of this group listed earlier in this chapter seem more appropriate to senior management. Surely their involvement and performance obligations are high, and might they not experience medium or high degrees of subordination?

Intuitively the term 'lower participants' seems to suggest those lowest in the organizational hierarchy. This interpretation is consistent with Etzioni's usage of the term but does not dispose of the difficulty in applying it to professional organizations. In colleges and hospitals are the lower participants junior teaching and medical staff or, are they blue collar porters, cleaners, caretakers and so on? It could even be argued that students and patients respectively constitute the lower participants.

The concept of congruence Fitting together.

Etzioni argues that organizations strive to maintain congruence through socialization and recruiting people compatible with the compliance structure. Yet organizations may have very little control over the cognitive and affective states of their members. There is evidence to suggest that people joining an organization move through a series of psychological states including depression (Adams, Hayes and Hopson, 1976); and, that individual development proceeds through phases and crises including drastic career reappraisal (Levinson, 1978). Arguably these affect a participant's responses to power and feelings of involvement. Recruitment does not guarantee congruence either,

18

as interviews (the most commonly used method of selection), are known to be poor predictors of personality and performance (e.g., Makin and Robertson, 1986). Arguably then, in practice congruency is harder to maintain than Etzioni suggests.

Concomitant relations between power and involvement

Etzioni's argument on power and involvement between different organizations and different levels of staff is open to question for several reasons. It could be argued that the reward and punishment structures appertaining to blue collar staff of factories, hospitals, colleges and professional organizations comprise more similarities than differences. This is because the ultimate sanction in all these organizations is dismissal whilst the number and scope of financial rewards are likely to be limited and similar. Etzioni suggests that control in colleges and hospitals for example, is more symbolic than in factories because it ultimately rests in the hands of professionals. The argument seems rather tenuous however as immediate supervisors of blue collar staff in these organizations are probably non-professionals promoted from the ranks.

As regards differences in the levels of power and involvement within organizations, whilst it is possible for example that private secretaries enjoy more status than ordinary clerks Etzioni does not explain why this means that the former tend to be a degree more symbolically controlled than the latter. His theory seems to rest on an assumption that autonomy and satisfaction are related to compliance structures.

Similarly Etzioni's view of senior staff as more symbolically controlled and more committed than the lower echelons may be flawed. The fact that they may enjoy more autonomy and greater reward does not obviate the possibility that rewards can be used coercively or, that autonomy may in practice be eradicated by high performance obligations which may also be experienced as coercion. Arguably then, control of senior

19

managers may actually be more coercive and intensive than for the lower echelons. Although Etzioni argues that senior managers tend to be more involved than lower participants, conceivably, the opposite is true. That is, because of their greater knowledge of the organization and decision making processes and outcomes, senior managers tend to become cynical discharging the letter rather than the spirit of their role.

Etzioni's theory of concomitant relationships between and within organizations implies that power is a linear phenomenon. Clegg (1989), however, argues that power relations in organizations are a constant struggle and one in which anything may be used as a resource. Whilst this does not dispose of the idea of concomitant variation, it does suggest that it may be inadequate to embrace the subtleties of power relations.

Is power a purely structural phenomenon?

Etzioni views power as emanating from the structure of organizations. This implies that the distribution of power is fixed and predictable and that its use in organizations is confined to attainment of goals.

This view is by no means universally accepted. Not all organizations are bureaucracies, especially some of Etzioni's extreme normative types. Many voluntary organizations for example do not possess formal role structures and other instruments of control. Indeed, certain radical organizations seek to reject the trappings of bureaucracy (e.g., Rothschild-Whitt, 1979: Baker, 1982). Yet all organizations need to mobilise power to attain their objectives for as Bierstedt (1950, p.784) argues, 'without power there is no organization.'

Even where operating within structurally defined limits powerholders invariably possess some autonomy (Lukes, 1974). People in power positions may acquire power beyond that which is structurally prescribed simply by assuming it (Martin, 1977), or, by manipulating and managing impressions of personal

20

power (Bacharach and Lawler, 1980).

This is because the reality of power depends partly upon an individual's perception. Power may succeed without a power holder possessing either the intention or the capability to reward or sanction, so long as the power subject believes in the reality of both (Bacharach and Lawler, 1980). This belief may lead someone to deduce the intentions of the power holder and comply with his wishes, solely on the basis of their own worst fears (Fisher and Ury, 1983).

Etzioni also seems to ignore the possibility that the nature of superior/subordinate relations may be perceived differently by individuals. For example, one employee may view a particular supervisor as friendly whereas another may see him as hostile. This is because in interacting people form images of one another; react to what they think the other person is feeling and thinking and may see the other as more powerful or sinister than they actually are. These feelings are not evident on any organization charts but are nonetheless real to those experiencing them (Heider, 1958; Brown, 1971; Mintroff, 1985).

This means that manipulation of rewards for example, may be experienced as coercion. This has obvious implications for measurement. It will be argued later that because perception is important, it is necessary to assess power from the standpoint of the power subject.

Another aspect of this debate concerns the distribution of power in organizations. Robbins (1983) has suggested that power in organizations can be understood as:

1 *Bases* - the resources power holders' possess.

2 *Forms* - the source of these resources.

3 *Tactics* - the way in which power is exercised.

Etzioni regards his three power types as resources arguing that their allocation is structurally determined. This seems to take rather a narrow view of power in organizations for a number of reasons. First, although structure may be a source of power, it is not the only one. Expertise, opportunity, personality and political competence can all be used to acquire resources and thereby create power (Bacharach and Lawler, 1980; Pfeffer, 1981).

Secondly, Etzioni disregards the various ways in which power may be exercised. The use of force, manipulation, influence and persuasion are not mentioned. These may be important because it is not always possible to mobilise formal power; for example, dismissal is constrained by law.

Finally there are purposes to which power is used in organizations. Etzioni implies that these are directly linked to the goals of the organization. Yet there is ample evidence to suggest that employees sometimes use their power to further their own interests, (e.g., Child, 1984; Stephenson, 1985; Pfeffer, 1992).

Etzioni's typology of power

Wrong (1979) argues that although different types of power may be treated as conceptually distinct, in reality they overlap. This means that power relations cannot be neatly classified and that, empirically, distinctions between various types of power are matters of degree. Whilst it is necessary to simplify concepts to construct theory, Wrong's arguments suggest that power relations do not fall readily into pre-determined categories as Etzioni suggests. It means that in measuring power, it is important to allow for overlap between the various types. This point is pursued in Chapter Eight.

Another aspect of Wrong's argument is the so called 'stock pile' theory of power. By this is meant the view that organizations, far from specialising in one type of power, seek to utilise as many forms as possible to take account of individuals' varying motivations to comply. Although this conflicts with Etzioni's power specialization theory, the two views are not irreconcilable. It is possible that given an arsenal of power, organizations nevertheless tend to rely upon one particular type.

Negative aspects of power

Control rests upon the ability to gratify or deny (Emerson, 1962). Etzioni's theory regarding utilitarian and normative organizations stresses gratification yet most organizational structures incorporate punishments as well as rewards (Child, 1984). Punishments (and rewards) may be administered arbitrarily and even in ignorance. As Handy (1985) notes, the presence of an overbearing boss can seem like coercion to his subordinates.

Etzioni defines coercion as the application of physical sanctions. This may explain why it is not emphasised in the context of utilitarian and normative organizations. Within the literature however, coercion is defined as a mental as well as a physical phenomenon.

Mental coercion may be defined as the deliberate infliction of emotional damage (Wrong, 1979). French and Raven (1968) view it as synonymous with punishment: for instance, the dismissal of an unsatisfactory employee. Similarly Bacharach and Lawler (1980) suggest coercion rests on fear of negative ramifications for failure to comply. Wrong argues that it is as injurious as damage to the body. Whether this is true or not is outside the scope of this research, what is important is that mental coercion is a factor within organizations and one which seems likely to affect involvement. It therefore forms part of the theoretical framework of this study.

Etzioni acknowledges that whilst lower participants possess some power it is invariably less than that of those in control. The question is, how much less? There is evidence to suggest that the lower echelons can acquire power out of all proportion to their role within the organization (Mechanic, 1962; Pettigrew, 1973). The reason for this resides partly in opportunity and partly in the reciprocal nature of power relations. Simmel (1950) suggests that although to outward appearances a power relation may seem like absolute domination matched by absolute submission, the reality is a complex interaction. All leaders are also led; for every exercise of power there exists a countervailing force (Galbraith, 1984). Possession of informal power may reify managerial intentions. A manager may have power to dismiss a subordinate but can be prevented from doing so if the subordinate is supported informally by others (Bierstedt, 1950). Likewise, Drummond (1991) recounts how a manager arbitrarily extended his share of floor space in an open plan office by moving his filing cabinets outwards. The staff secretly moved them back and inch or so every day until the manager eventually ended up with eighteen inches less space than he had originally without every realising what had happened!

Informal power is by no means confined to such localised incidents. A major source of lower participant power is dependency. Dependency is thought to be most relevant in the execution of decisions when the organization must rely upon employees as agents of its will (Mintzberg, 1983). Lammers (1988, p.439) expresses some of the possibilities for subversion, 'A directive . . . may have to be transferred and translated (reformulated, elaborated, operationalized) several times before it reaches its destination and becomes implemented. Such processes . . . provide some scope for detaining, deflecting, or diluting.' Even where employees behave with impunity, the organization may be unable to exert control. Sterba (1978), for example, notes how the Chinese civil service was dependent upon local recruitment to staff it's clerical posts. The clerks exploited their unique knowledge gleaned over generations to frustrate their superiors by tactics such as delay, preoccupation with petty details and selective amnesia.

Secondary sources of power

There is a contradiction in Etzioni's theory between his assertion that organizations utilise secondary forms of power and his statement that a prisoner doing a favour for a guard in return for a cigarette is being subjected to coercive not remunerative power. Does this mean that praising an employee in a utilitarian organization is an exercise of remunerative not symbolic power because the value of praise lies in its implications for material reward at some point?

The contradiction seems unresolvable. Perhaps though it should not detract from the central tenet of Etzioni's theory, that is the tendency of organizations to depend upon one type of power. It is on this that the research focuses.

The definition of involvement

It was noted earlier that Etzioni defines involvement as an actor's cathectic evaluative orientation. It is not clear what this actually means, what involvement is, or how it can be observed. The only clue is contained in a footnote (Etzioni, 1975, p.9), where he indicates that it relates to a person's orientation towards the organization. Otherwise one is left to deduce from his usage of the term and his review of research into compliance variables as to what he means by involvement. In fact, Etzioni's concept of involvement identifies closely with the psychological literature on organizational commitment, the subject of the next chapter.

Conclusions

It might be argued that if Etzioni's theory is so flawed conceptually then research is pointless. The case for an empirical investigation is as follows. First, as Glaser and Strauss (1968) point out, argument does not destroy a theory. It may identify weaknesses and inadequacies but these can form the basis of inter-theoretical bridge building resulting in an improvement of the original.

  Second, although objections have been raised against certain aspects of Etzioni's theory, the evidence in support of these objections is no more substantial than that underlying Etzioni's assertions. For example the claim and counter claim relating to the level of involvement of senior staff are not based upon data of any kind. Potentially both views appeal to common sense even though they appear to be diametrically opposed. It is argued that the only way to resolve an issue such as this is by empirical examination.

  Third, the literature upon power is extremely complex. A major strength of Etzioni's theory is that its treatment of power is simple and therefore potentially more useful than some of the more complicated models. Moreover, the fact that it does not, for example, encompass more aspects of organizational power does not mean that it can never do so. Empirical validation and/or qualification of the basic theory might pave the way for development not only of Etzioni's theory, but also in relation to power in organizations generally. Likewise research into Etzioni's theory can potentially contribute to the literature on organizational commitment.

2 The nature of involvement

Introduction

Etzioni (1975, p.18) defines involvement as 'The cathectic evaluative orientation of an actor to an object.' Within the literature, the concept of involvement has two meanings. Firstly it may be viewed as a psychological attachment evidenced by the willingness of participants to devote energy and loyalty to the organization (Kanter, 1968). The second aspect of involvement concerns the investments made by individuals as a result of their membership of the organization (Becker, 1960). This behaviourial view of involvement suggests that as time goes on, it becomes increasingly difficult for individuals to leave the organization because of their accumulated investments.

The literature is potentially confusing because the terms involvement, alienation and commitment are used interchangeably. This is often compounded by the association of organizational involvement with overlapping constructs such as satisfaction, work involvement and so on. It is therefore necessary to differentiate between the various terms and their meanings before proceeding to examine involvement in more detail. This is accomplished in two stages: first by examining the relationship between generalised concepts of work alienation and involvement; second by defining and clarifying organizational involvement in relation to concepts of work involvement.

The relationship between alienation and involvement

The term alienation is derived from the original Latin noun meaning *alienatio* which in turn is derived from the Latin verb, *alienare* meaning to 'take away' or 'remove'. The Latin usage of the term in two different contexts resulted in two meanings. The first pertains to transfer of ownership, the second meaning is 'to cause separation'.

Kanungo (1982) argues that defining alienation as a state of separation implies:

1   Alienation from some thing.

2   Feelings of hostility, indifference and aversion towards the object of alienation.

Etzioni defines alienation as an intensely negative attitude towards the organization. Although it has many meanings within the literature, most definitions of alienation include some or all of the facets identified by Seeman (1959). These are:

1   *Powerlessness* - the belief held by an individual that his own behaviour cannot determine events.

2   *Meaninglessness* - where the individual cannot be certain about what he ought to believe.

3   *Normlessness* - the breakdown of social norms regulating conduct.

4   *Isolation* - where the individual becomes estranged from his society and its cultures.

5   *Self-estrangement* - where a person experiences himself as alien.

Four of Seeman's five factors pertain to the individual. Normlessness, the third factor pertains to the societal level.

Kanungo (1979, 1982) has argued (with empirical support, e.g., Leftkowitz and Brigando, 1980), that alienation and involvement are opposite sides of the same concept. Viewing it in this way, argues Kanungo, sociologists have tended to use the phenomenon as a negative concept whereas psychologists have looked upon it positively. Psychologists Kanungo suggests, have focused upon the benefits of involvement though without considering what it means to be uninvolved. Sociologists have concentrated on the presence of alienation, without explaining the unalienated experience.

Etzioni regards alienation as a negative form of involvement and, the emphasis of his work is upon involvement in organizations rather than alienation from them. In any case, Etzioni (1975) has indicated that for practical purposes it is valid to treat involvement as a uni-dimensional concept. For these reasons this study concentrates upon involvement in organizations.

Involvement related concepts

Etzioni focuses upon members' orientation to the organization though his theory embraces involvement related concepts which have subsequently become confused within the literature. Morrow (1983) analyzed construct definitions, operational definitions and measures of involvement related concepts, seeking to clarify these and identify areas of concept redundancy. She noted there are over twenty-five of these but suggested they can be divided into six reasonably discrete forms.

The 'Protestant work ethic' focuses on values, and is concerned with the intrinsic worth of work as an end in itself. It is based on the extent to which a person feels that his or her personal worth results from self-sacrificing work or occupational achievement. 'Job involvement' centres on the degree of absorption in work activity. It can be defined as the extent to which a person is identified psychologically with work, and the degree to which work performance affects their self-esteem. 'Central Life Interest' (Dubin, 1956) focuses on the degree to which a person's job is central to their lives. It measures whether a person is job-orientated, is not job-orientated or neutral. A fourth form of work commitment is 'career salience' focusing on the perceived importance of work and career in a person's life as a whole. 'Union commitment', the fifth category, is concerned with devotion and loyalty to one's trades union. It is measured as the extent to which a person desires to remain a member of the union, to exert effort on behalf of the union, and to identify with its objectives. Finally there is 'organizational commitment' which is based on devotion and loyalty to the employing organization. Morrow concludes that organizational commitment suffers least from the problem of overlap based as it is on attachment to the organization. The other five forms of involvement are more concerned with attitudes to work and therefore are bound to be related to one another.

Rabinowitz and Hall (1977) attribute the problem of overlap to integration between concepts. They argue for example that a person exposed to the Protestant work ethic is almost certain to exhibit high levels of job involvement. Morrow (1983) takes a similar line. Morrow says that it is hardly surprising that Central Life Interest and career salience overlap. Individuals whose work is central to them are unlikely to feel their careers are unimportant.

Concept redundancy has also been created by the difficulties in measuring concepts. Researchers faced either with variability in the concept not captured in the measures, or, with variability in the measures not reflected in the concept, have responded by creating new measures out of old items. This only seemed to exacerbate the problem (Schneider, 1985).

Organizational commitment, concludes Morrow, is the most independent of the six forms of involvement. However, although measures succeed in maintaining an organizational focus, the potential for overlap exists as the various forms of work involvement correlate with organizational commitment (Morrow and Melroy, 1986). It will be argued later however that the relationship should not be dismissed as a tautology. This is because if organizational involvement is systematically related to organizations, and if work involvement (or alienation) is related to organizational involvement, then it suggests the latter might also vary systematically between organizations. This argument and its implications for measurement are pursued in Chapters Five and Six.

The importance of involvement

Etzioni (1975) states that in order to realise their goals, organizations require the positive orientation of participants to power. Kanter (1968) shares Etzioni's view of the importance of involvement. She argues that social orders are supported by people and that the problem of organizations is to ensure that participants become positively involved. Ideally, involvement needs to be based on more than simple material exchange. This has been emphasised by Smith, Organ and Near (1983) in a study of organizational citizenship behaviour. They note that organizations often need to rely upon altruism and spontaneous, unrewarded help from employees. Katz (1964) observed that innovative behaviours going beyond role prescriptions are essential for the functioning of an organization. Even where work is highly routinised, the organization is nevertheless dependent upon the exercise of workers' 'tacit skills' in maintaining production (e.g., Leplat, 1990; Wood, 1990). This

31

implies that it is to the organization's advantage to foster high levels of involvement and so reduce the need for control and the cost of providing material inducements.

The nature of involvement

This section describes the two concepts of involvement known as attitudinal and behaviourial respectively. Of the two, the latter has attracted most attention. It seeks to describe how individuals come to think about and evaluate their relationship with the organization. The behaviourial concept of involvement views it as a process whereby individuals become committed to the organization in the sense that they choose to remain not so much because they want to, but because they have become 'locked in' as a result of their behaviours.

Attitudinal involvement

Attitudinal involvement essentially concerns an individual's psychological attachment to the organization. There are many definitions in the literature; for example, those of Buchanan (1974), Cook and Wall (1980), Mowday, Porter and Steers (1982) and Morrow (1983). Most contain one or more of the following elements:

1   A desire to remain a member of the organization.

2   A willingness to exert high levels of effort on behalf of the organization.

3   A belief in, and acceptance, of the values and goals of the organization.

Kelman (1958) proposed three levels of attachment, based on the degree to which the individual internalises perspectives of the organization. Kelman suggests individuals accept influence in three ways, compliance, identification and internalization. Compliance occurs when attitudes and behaviours are adopted simply to gain specific rewards. An individual does what is required of him but may retain his private thoughts on the matter. Identification occurs when an individual accepts influence to establish or maintain a satisfying relationship, such as membership of a group. Here an individual may respect the group's values without adopting them as his own. Internalization occurs when influence is accepted because the induced attitudes and behaviours are congruent with one's own values. That is, individual and group values are identical.

These three psychological states represent three dimensions of involvement. Compliance rests on calculative involvement for rewards. Identification is based on a desire for affiliation, whilst internalization reflects congruence between individual and organizational values.

Kanter's concept of involvement is also based on identification of individual interests with those of the organization: She defines it as, 'A process through which individual interests become attached to the carrying out of socially organized patterns of behaviour which are seen as fulfilling those interests and expressing the nature and needs of the person,' (Kanter, 1968, p.499).

This process, says Kanter, involves three separate problems; social control, group cohesiveness and retention of participants. These are analytically distinct, a participant may be committed to maintaining membership of an organization but occasionally ill-behaved within it; the inmate of a prison may develop close ties with other inmates, but wish to leave at the earliest opportunity.

Each facet of commitment argues Kanter, is related to cognitive, cathectic or calculative evaluation of the costs of remaining or leaving. Cohesion-commitment or group solidarity depends on participants forming cathectic orientations. That is, they form ties binding them to the community which then result in feelings of gratification on being members of a group. Control-commitment is the willingness of participants to uphold norms and obey the authority of the group. It rests on their forming positive evaluative orientations, 'Demands made by the system are evaluated as right, as moral, as just, as expressing one's own values, so that obedience to these demands is a normative necessity and sanctioning by the system is regarded as appropriate, (Kanter, 1968, p.514).

The process of commitment can thus be viewed on a scale. It begins with cognition, where obedience is on the basis of a member's evaluation of potential rewards and punishments. At the middle stage of the process, obedience results from the forming of social attachments to others (cohesion-commitment). Finally obedience rests on an internalized moral code.

Kelman, Kanter and Etzioni's models of involvement consist of three levels, the highest of which is the internalized acceptance of values. This seems to imply that internalized acceptance is the most desirable form of involvement for organizations to achieve though it is not clear for what purpose or for whom. Although many organization cultures are orientated to the attainment of high levels of employee involvement, there are many more successful organizations which are not. It could also be argued that although occasionally organizations may need employees to go beyond the call of duty, by and large provided they discharge their role obligations satisfactorily, no greater level of involvement is actually necessary.

Another approach is one based on exchange whereby members of an organization contribute in return for inducements (Simon, 1957). This view of involvement is related to equity theory (Adams, 1965). The concept of equity is based on social exchanges characterised by reciprocity and social comparison processes. In the context of organizations, people compare their efforts

and sacrifices with those of others and expect a fair rewa
return. Fair means being neither under nor over rewa...
What is important is that inputs and outputs are perceived as
balancing. Inequity arises where the balance is perceived as
distorted. This creates dissatisfaction and anger, motivating
participants to restore equity by some means, for example,
lowering inputs, restructuring their perception of the situation,
leaving or forcing the other party to leave.

Similarly commitment can be viewed as an expression of the
psychological contract (Schein, 1980). This may be defined as
the extent to which employee and organizational expectations
are met in a relationship where each party trades something in
return for something of value to the other. Relating the concept
of the psychological contract to Etzioni's theories, Schein
suggests 'fair' contracts are similar to Etzioni's congruent
compliance structures and unfair, or violated contracts, as
identifying with incongruent structures.

Employees come to the organization with expectations. Where
these are fulfilled commitment results. The reverse also applies.
The psychological contract is constantly renegotiated as the
employer relies on power to enforce his side whilst the employee
can reduce his involvement in work, or resort to sabotage, to
enforce the employer's compliance (Steers, 1977).   Mowday's
(1979) review of equity theory highlighted a number of
weaknesses particularly restoration of equity where
overpayment exists. The review also produced evidence to
suggest that far from being the fulcrum of exchange in social
relationships, equity is actually just one of the norms governing
the distribution of rewards.

Another difficulty with these so called 'exchange' models of
commitment is that they do not appear to take much account of
the role of power in organizations. In many work situations it
would be difficult if not impossible for an employee to reduce
or even increase outputs. Moreover strikes and sabotage tend
to be risky and costly courses of action. The idea that the

psychological contract involves mutual trade off seems to imply a relationship between equals. Yet Marx argues that there is a vast power differential between employer and employee. Moreover in a coercive organization, the inequality of power relations is even more pronounced.

Involvement as a behaviour

So far involvement has been viewed mainly as an attitude. This approach emphasises the process by which employees come to think about and to evaluate their relationship with the organization. Behaviourial involvement is a process by which people come to be bound by their own past actions. In this context involvement means accounting for '. . . the fact that people engage in a consistent line of activity,' (Becker, 1960, p.32)

The 'line of activity' of interest here is continued membership of an organization. However, this so called investments model of involvement has been applied quite widely and includes friendship and romantic associations (Rusbult, 1980a,b) and the escalation of commitment to a course of action in decision making (Staw, 1981).

Becker suggests that consistency of behaviour can be explained by what he calls the making of 'side-bets' or investments which make it difficult to leave say a marriage or abandon a particular course of action. In organizations people become committed by mixing their extraneous interests with their employment. Eventually these past actions or side-bets make the consequences of inconsistency more expensive than consistency. Quite often, involvement in the organization alone is sufficient to create side-bets. For example, cultural expectations that an employee should remain with an employer for two to three years may deter someone from taking up the offer of a better job within months of joining the organization. What Becker calls 'impersonal bureaucratic arrangements' of organizations may

36

also create side-bets for employees, for example pension schemes, penalizing early leavers. These are sometimes referred to as the 'golden handcuffs.'

Just as there may be congruency between employee attitudes and the organization's fulfilment of expectations, congruency may also exist between attitudes and behaviours. Salancik (1977) argues that commitment can be a powerful factor in shaping attitudes because people adjust them to fit the situations to which they are committed. A self-reinforcing cycle emerges leading to further committing attitudes, and corresponding changes in behaviour and so on. Each sustains the other, as employees develop committing behaviours they develop attitudes consistent with those behaviours.

Binding behaviours, says Salancik, have four characteristics. Firstly, the behaviour must be explicit, unambiguous and undeniable. Secondly, it must be irrevocable or extremely difficult to change. Third, the decision must be public. Finally, the decision must have been reached on the employee's own volition. When job choices are characterised by these factors, then, says Salancik, employees will become behaviourially committed to the decision. The commitment is likely to be positive to enable individuals to justify it.

It could be argued of course that it is not only investments within the organization which commit people to staying. For example someone with a strong Protestant Work Ethic might feel constrained from taking up an alternative life style. Indeed as far as coercive organizations are concerned, it is behaviour outside the organization that actually results in committal.

Involvement as an attitude and a behaviour

Mowday, et al. (1982) argue that if involvement is to be fully understood, there is little point in looking either to attitudes or behaviours as causes. They suggest it is more useful to regard the two as reciprocally related over time. That is, attitudes lead

37

to committing behaviours, which reinforce attitudes, and committing behaviours lead to commitment attitudes and subsequent committing behaviours. They argue that it matters not whether the process begins with either attitude or behaviour. What is important is the recognition that the development of involvement involves a subtle interplay of the two over time.

The dynamics of involvement

Mowday et al. (1982) identify three phases in the development of involvement: anticipation (pre-employment), initiation and entrenchment. Involvement develops through and is affected by employment experience at each of these stages.

The major determinant of involvement during the early employment period consists of pre-employment experiences such as job expectations, job choice factors and on employees personal characteristics. Initial work experiences such as the job itself, supervision, work group, pay and the organization are also important. Initial work experiences that reduce an employee's feeling of responsibility are likely to reduce involvement (Salancik, 1977).

Mowday et al. argue that as time goes on, side-bets become an increasingly important determinant of involvement. This is because as investments, social involvement, decreased job mobility and earlier sacrifices accumulate, it becomes more difficult for an employee to leave the organization.

Functional and dysfunctional aspects of involvement

It has been suggested that involvement is important to organizations because it can generate contributions from the employee over and above his contractual obligations. Its special value is that where it results from the internalised acceptances of organizational goals, it need not be purchased.

The unprofitable side of involvement has not received much attention from researchers (Griffin and Bateman, 1986). The implication within the literature is that more is better (Randall, 1987). Mowday et al. (1982) suggest ineffective employees may choose to remain with the organization because their previous behaviours have committed them. Over-involved zealots may become an embarrassment. Employees who become entrenched may also block change because of their misplaced loyalty. In stressful situations, an employee with commitments outside the organization can be less damaging than one whose whole identity is invested with it.

Randall (1987) suggests that a moderate level of commitment is the most desirable one for organizations to achieve. Moderate means a state where employees exhibit sufficient cooperation and goodwill to enable the organization to respond to crises but without subsuming their entire existence to it. Interestingly this is precisely the level of involvement which Etzioni suggests is appropriate in utilitarian organizations.

Multiple involvements

Brown (1969) has suggested that identification is exclusive. The selection of an object for identification depends partly on its isolation from other social alternatives, and partly on its special qualities. Reichers (1985) has taken the opposite stance. She argues that the concept of organizational commitment is insensitive, referring as it does to the organization as a whole. Individuals experience multiple commitments to all aspects of organizations, co-workers, top management, work group, department, professional association and so on.

Involvement therefore needs to be understood as a collection of multiple attachments experienced simultaneously and variously by the individuals who make up organizations.

Organizations are not single entities but composed of coalitions and constituencies. These coalitions may have goals which differ from one another. Yet, argues Reichers, existing conceptualizations of organizational commitment speak of identification with organizational goals, though it is unlikely that members all share the same goals. Instead, specific groups and their goals should be identified as the focus for the multiple commitments which individuals experience.

Reichers notes that there is evidence to suggest that professionals experience conflicting commitments between professional and organizational goals. Union members too she argues may experience dual allegiance to their employing organization and union. Whereas theorists and researchers have viewed involvement as an attachment to the organization, the organization is an abstract concept. For most employees, reality is represented by co-workers, supervisors, subordinates, customers and so on. Involvement therefore should be re-conceptualised from a general to a more specific construct to reflect multiple commitments of multiple groups which form the organization.

One aspect of multiple involvements which Reichers does not emphasise is the boundaries of an organization. Arguably for example, inmates not only feel hostile towards the prison alone but the whole penal system including police, lawyers, courts and so on which they may see as being responsible for their incarceration. A Civil Servant may at various points identify with the Civil Service as a whole, a specific branch or a particular department or any combination of these. Likewise does a member of say the Red Cross feel committed to their particular branch, or the whole organization, or both?

Work involvement and work alienation

It was said earlier in this chapter that work involvement (or alienation) is another important concept in this study. It is therefore necessary to examine it in more detail. It was also suggested earlier that the concepts of involvement and alienation are polar opposites. The same argument has also been applied to work involvement and work alienation (Kanungo, 1979).

Whereas psychologists' interest in work involvement is relatively recent, the study of work alienation has a long tradition amongst sociologists. Although the phenomenon tends to be associated with post-industrialization, theologians and philosophers have regarded it as a human experience since the beginning of mankind. Since the dark ages, magic and mysticism have influenced man's attempts to produce and maintain a living. Theologians attributed spiritual alienation to material involvement and so encouraged work alienation if work was a means of satisfying personal material needs. Likewise in Hindu scripture, work was considered desirable only when it was performed out of a sense of duty without desire for personal gain or attachment to its outcomes (Kaufmann, 1970; Kanungo, 1982).

Contemporary thinking on work alienation has been strongly influenced by Marx. Previously philosophers and theologians identified alienation with man's spiritual condition. Marx associated it with man's working life. For Marx, alienation of workers refers to a state of separation from labour (and its products) and loss of autonomy and control. Most industrial work settings according to Marx provided job conditions that alienated workers rather than involved them. To Marx, the division of labour means that work has no individual character; it becomes simple and monotonous, the worker a mere appendage of a machine.

Blauner (1964) has applied Seeman's (1959) dimensions of alienation to work. In this context powerlessness relates to the

41

extent of worker's control over their conditions of employment. Meaninglessness refers to the significance a product has for a worker. Isolation is the absence of membership of an industrial community and self estrangement occurs when work is deprived of feelings of wholeness and identity.

Work alienation then centres upon separation from work. Work involvement stresses identification with it. Work involvement may be defined as 'psychological absorbtion with one's work' (Lawler and Hall, 1970). It reflects the degree to which a person's job is central to their identity. According to Lodahl and Kejner (1965), work involvement reflects ego involvement in one's job and psychological identification with work.

Causes of work alienation and work involvement

Reviewing the research, Kanungo (1982) noted both work alienation and work involvement share the same preconditions. Fulfilment of intrinsic needs through individual freedom, power and control contribute to low alienation or high involvement. For example, Blauner (1964) linked work alienation with technology observing that it was higher where technology afforded the worker least control over his environment and least prestige. Similarly Trist and Bamforth (1951) noted a loss of meaning in work for miners when traditional work groups were broken up following a change in methods of coal extraction.

Psychologists have emphasised that satisfaction of self esteem needs lead to work involvement. This refers to fulfilment of needs to achieve, to belong, a sense of pride, experience of personal success and so on (Vroom, 1962; Patchen, 1970). Management can facilitate need fulfilment by designing appropriate systems of communication and control. Participation for example, with its emphasis on shared decision making and involvement is associated with enhanced quality of working life (Chell, 1985). Equally management can create the opposite. According to McGregor (1960), managers subscribing to Theory X often create conditions within the organization which alienate employees.

The interchangeability of preconditions is summarily expressed by Maslow (1954). He argues that satisfaction of self esteem needs leads to feelings of self-confidence, adequacy and purposefulness. Frustration of these needs results in feelings of inferiority, weakness and helplessness.

The argument then is that by creating appropriate conditions, management can foster self esteem and consequently greater work involvement. Yet nowhere is it suggested that enhanced work involvement leads to higher productivity. Indeed it could be argued that loss of meaning in work does not necessarily mean loss of production or a lowering of standards, yet there seems to be an implication that self actualization (whatever it might mean) is good. Moreover because it is 'good' there is also the implication that management has a responsibility to enhance the quality of working life without considering the costs in relation to benefits. For example, employee participation schemes cost money to operate yet there is no firm evidence that participation leads to increased satisfaction or productivity (Wall and Lischeron, 1977). Furthermore it is conceivable that the reverse could result through lost time and workers' feelings of powerlessness if their participation does not result in change.

Discussion and conclusions

One general criticism emerging from this review is that most of the writers have focused on employing organizations as distinct from coercive, voluntary and cooperative types. As regards organizational involvement, theorists have tended to concentrate upon attitudinal involvement though it seems that the investments model could explain much about why people choose to remain or come to feel trapped within organizations.

Yet apart from Becker's paper, very little work on behaviourial involvement exists. Also, Morrow's (1983) review of the relationship between organizational involvement and forms of work involvement and Reicher's (1985) paper on multiple involvements both highlight the need for considerable conceptual integration and development.

As far as this research topic is concerned, this review suggests involvement is a dynamic phenomenon influenced by many variables besides power. Particularly significant is the so called 'side bets' aspect of involvement. It is possible to imagine that people in coercive and voluntary organizations make investments (e.g., good conduct, social standing), but it seems reasonable to suggest that involvement in employing organizations may be more influenced by this factor as investments are more numerous. This might mean that in employing organizations, the relationship between power and involvement is more tenuous than in non employing organizations.

Etzioni emphasises attitudinal involvement. It could therefore be argued that his theory is incomplete as it fails to take account of the consequences of so called 'side bets'. It seems though that the distinction between attitudes and behaviour in this context is blurred anyway. Constructs of attitudinal involvement such as willingness to stay and exert effort are expressed as behaviours. An individual may nurse the attitude that he would leave the organization tomorrow if he could find another job but choose to remain because of lack of alternatives. Hence though his behaviour is calculative, his attitude towards the organization is hostile.

It is interesting that internalization is stressed as the ideal form of involvement in employing organizations. This equates with Etzioni's concept of moral involvement which he suggests is only to be found in normative organizations. Yet if moral involvement is a prerequisite of self sacrifice and sublime performance, then it seems unlikely that employing

44

organizations will not attempt to generate it somehow especially as symbolic reward is an extremely cost effective means of engendering commitment. This would suggest that in utilitarian organizations, symbolic and remunerative power are likely to be mixed, perhaps more so than Etzioni's theory would suggest. So little is known about multiple involvements in organizations that any comment here must be purely speculative. There seem to be two possibilities. The first is that they may act as moderators of the relationship between power and involvement. The second is that they may actually relate systematically to compliance structures. An individual who is positively orientated towards the organization is more likely to be committed to co-workers, management and so on.

It is also pertinent to reflect upon Etzioni's choice of organizational involvement as the second major variable. The literature reviewed here suggests that individuals experience many forms of involvement and it is a debatable as to which might be the most significant determinant of effectiveness. It could be argued for example that work involvement has more bearing on productivity than an individual's attitude to the organization.

Part of the function of this chapter has been to differentiate between organizational involvement and related concepts appertaining to work involvement. The intention was to prepare the way for a review of research into compliance variables and to set the stage for development of the research model. This in fact incorporates work alienation as new correlate. The rationale for this is developed in Chapters Five and Six.

3 The sociological literature on compliance in organizations

Introduction

Etzioni's theory was derived partly by deduction from theoretical premises and partly by induction from empirical data (Etzioni, 1975). According to Etzioni, the latter involved analysis of hundreds of empirical studies of what he loosely terms compliance variables. These include not only power and involvement, but also wider concepts such as alienation, work involvement and satisfaction.

The purpose of this chapter is to review the research concerning compliance variables, and to critically evaluate whether, and to what extent, they support Etzioni's theory. In his own appraisal of compliance studies, Etzioni (1975) commented that none of the research was pursued in a co-ordinated manner and therefore the literature lacks cohesion. This has not changed consequently, this review is inevitably fragmented. To impose some order and make the material intelligible, the chapter is divided into two sections. The first reviews studies which test the core theory. The second covers research which has examined a particular aspect of Etzioni's theory such as the relationship between power and involvement, or the relationship between compliance structures and effectiveness.

Tests of Etzioni's core theory

There are few studies of Etzioni's compliance theory. Those that exist variously confirm and disconfirm Etzioni's ideas, though it is argued that much of the research reviewed in this section suffers from methodological weaknesses which render the conclusions of many studies suspect.

Franklin (1975) studied white and blue collar staff in six organizations, two newspapers, a general hospital, a small manufacturing plant, a creamery and a public service organization. The study focused on the relationship between power, involvement and task performance. Power was operationalised by asking supervisors and employees to rate their preferred power tactics (Mann and Dent, 1954). Items such as: 'Give pat on the back' and 'Give more interesting work' represented symbolic power, and items on promotions and pay increases represented remunerative power. Involvement was operationalised as: willingness to uphold organizational norms, and willingness to remain with the organization. Task performance was operationalised by utilising supervisor's appraisal notes. Lower participants were defined as staff in non-supervisory positions.

Franklin defined the newspaper companies and hospital as normative structures, but found that all six organizations relied more on remunerative than symbolic power. Involvement was higher in organizations defined as normative than in those classified as utilitarian, though this only applied to white collar staff. Relationships between power and task performance, and involvement and task performance, were negligible.

It is not surprising that Franklin found no differences in power between the six organizations as his methodology is questionable. Asking supervisors what tactics they find effective does not necessarily reveal which they actually use. Furthermore, employees were asked to rank which methods of control they preferred, this is not the same as asking how they are actually

48

controlled. In other words, it could be said that Franklin does not actually measure power at all. Nor is it surprising that the study revealed no differences in the level of involvement amongst blue collar staff as the band of organizations studied was very narrow and consequently their compliance structures were probably very similar. For example, a newspaper is arguably a utilitarian organization, not a normative one. Had a coercive and/or an extreme normative organization been included, then the results might have been different.

Warren (1968) examined the power structure of eighteen schools plus relationships between power, and behavioural and attitudinal conformity, of teachers. Power was based upon French and Raven's typology measured as follows:

1   *Coercion* - teachers' perceptions of their supervisors as authoritarian.

2   *Reward* - supervisors' allocation of desirable jobs.

3   *Expert* - rating of supervisors as logical and rational.

4   *Legitimate* - rating of supervisors as items such as 'fair'   and 'conscientious'.

5   *Referent* - extent of teacher's satisfaction with school.

Behavioral conformity was operationalised as the degree to which teachers used approaches preferred by the principal. Attitudinal conformity was measured by teachers' perception of their level of responsibility. Warren (p.968) concluded first that; 'Our findings do not support a linear relationship between a given form of power and effective social control,' and second that, 'Power bases may not be mutually exclusive, yet this is a tenet of Etzioni's tripartite analysis of organizational forms.'

The first conclusion is based on the fact that attitudinal and behaviourial conformity correlated differently with the five forms of power. For example, coercive and reward power were more strongly related to behaviourial than attitudinal conformity. Expert and legitimate power were more closely associated with attitudinal conformity, whilst referent power was positively correlated with both types of conformity. The second conclusion relates to inter-correlations between the five types of power. Coercive and reward power tended to occur together, and referent power was highly correlated with all other bases.

Although Warren suggested his evidence contradicts Etzioni's theory, there are theoretical and methodological issues which need to be considered in interpreting these results. Warren operationalised French and Raven's typology of power, not Etzioni's. It is clear that there are wide differences between for example, Etzioni's concept of remunerative power and Warren's operationalisation of the construct. Warren's items measuring referent power (satisfaction, feelings of unity, and willingness to stay), are actually more akin to involvement and therefore it is perhaps not surprising that they correlate with the other four forms of power some of which were measured using only one item. Furthermore, Warren measured conformity not involvement. Conformity is perhaps a manifestation of involvement, but it is only a manifestation, Warren cannot therefore be said to have operationalised involvement directly. Indeed, the correlations between various types of power and conformity are actually consistent with Etzioni's general argument. For example, is it surprising that coercion and reward should elicit only ostensible (behaviourial) conformity, whereas referent power should be related to both attitudes and behaviour?

As regards Warren's second conclusion, it is not true that Etzioni does not allow for power mixes. Etzioni argues that organizations use all three forms of control, but tend to rely upon one particular type. Besides, Etzioni classifies schools as dual organizations relying equally upon symbolic power and coercion. Consequently inter-correlations amongst power bases are inevitable.

In later studies based on French and Raven's constructs, expert and referent power bases were positively associated compliance and satisfaction whereas legitimate power correlated only with compliance (Rahim, 1989; Rahim and Buntman, 1989). Coercion was not significantly related to compliance or satisfaction. Although this study apparently both confirms and disconfirms Etzioni's theory, the validity of the power measures is questionable. Power is operationalised as the availability of rewards and sanctions rather than their actual use. For example, 'My superior can fire me if my performance is consistently below standards,' (p.550). What a supervisor can do says little about what a supervisor will do or what a subordinate believes a supervisor may do.

Boettecher (1973) criticised Etzioni for failing to allow for multiple power relations as a result of a study of power and involvement in public welfare agency. This revealed an equal reliance upon symbolic and remunerative power though neither type of power correlated with involvement which was measured as the use, or non use, of food stamps. Boettecher suggested that this might have been a reflection of the neutralising effect of the dual power structure, but it is doubtful whether the method used to measure involvement is adequate and this alone might account for the results. Boettecher defined the agency as a normative organization and argued that existence of a dual power structure contradicts Etzioni's theory. Besides, power was measured from the standpoint of the agency workers, and not the clients, whose perceptions might have been quite different.

Pearce (1983) also concluded that his evidence disconfirmed Etzioni's theory. Pearce hypothesised that leaders in utilitarian organizations would exert more influence than their counterparts in voluntary normative ones, as Etzioni's theory implies tighter control in utilitarian structures. In fact, the results showed the opposite. Voluntary leaders' willingness to expend time and energy enabled them to develop an influential role by default of the passive membership of the majority, and freedom from of government pressure hindering their paid counterparts.

Contrary to Pearce's conclusions, his results may in fact support Etzioni's theory. Etzioni argues that normative organizations rely on expressive leadership, and therefore leaders are more likely to use influence tactics than formal, or 'tight' control. Pearce's findings seem to substantiate this. Further evidence suggests that high member involvement in normative organizations guarantees compliance and therefore obviates the need for directive leadership provided members feel they are involved in the organization and can exert some control over its activities (Houghland, Shepard and Wood, 1979; Houghland and Wood, 1980). For example, Wood (1975) found that church leaders could pursue normative goals such as social justice, to which members were not necessarily committed, but acquiesced because of their high involvement in the church. Similarly Torres, McIntosh and Zey (1991) noted that volunteers were more concerned with participation in operational rather than policy decisions. Interestingly participation in decision making was a more significant predictor of their willingness to donate time and energy than organizational commitment.

Three studies which Etzioni (1975) claims support his theory are, Julian (1966 and 1968), and Miller (1967). Julian studied the compliance structure of five hospitals. Involvement was measured on the basis of patients' feelings toward staff sanctions. Power was measured by patients' statements about staff conduct. In accordance with Etzioni's theory, the results indicated a preponderance of positive involvement and symbolic power. Coercive sanctions correlated highly with negative involvement. However the relationship between symbolic power and positive involvement was weak. Julian suggested this might be accounted for by the amount of control - that is, the greater the control, be it coercive or symbolic, the lower the level of positive involvement.

Although Julian's work confirms Etzioni's theory in part, the use of unvalidated measures limits the extent to which inferences can be reliably drawn from it. Also, Julian focuses upon only one kind of organization and therefore does not really address the central issue of power and involvement between the three types of organization.

Miller observed that work alienation was lower in a science laboratory described as an atmosphere more akin to a university than a traditional research and development department of the same organization. The study also showed the more utilitarian the incentives, and more direct the control, the higher the level of work alienation. Etzioni (1975) claims that these results support his theory because they demonstrate that the university like laboratory was a normative organization whereas the other exemplified a utilitarian structure. Yet there is no evidence to suggest that the difference in levels of alienation were linked to power since this was not measured in the study. Also, in referring to alienation, Etzioni does not take account of the fact that Miller measured work alienation, not organizational alienation. Therefore whilst the results might suggest a relationship between power and involvement, they do no more than that.

Compliance in extreme normative organizations

Another approach to compliance theory is to examine how organizations seek to foster intense commitment. Adler and Adler (1988) studied the development of intense loyalty is a sport's team. The author's definition of loyalty corresponds closely with Etzioni's concept of moral involvement, 'Feelings of attachment, of belonging, of strongly wanting to be part of something; . . . the readiness to contribute part of oneself with the group, and . . . to follow faithfully the leadership or guidelines of the organization,' (p. 401).

Five factors emerged as critical to the development of intense loyalty. First, domination by a strong leader, in this case the team coach. Second, identification, in this case encouraging team members to act as organizational representatives and rewarding them accordingly. Third, fostering commitment by focusing upon individuals' feelings of performance and investment. Fourth, integration, that is, developing a high level of group cohesion. This was partly achieved isolating the group from outside contacts and by encouraging hostility to other groups. Fifth, goal alignment, that is, convincing individuals that their own goals could best be attained by pursuit of the team's goals. Interestingly developing intense loyalty involves stimulating negative emotions as well as positive emotions. Domination, for example, is achieved through athletes' dependency upon coach for their needs. Dependency ranges from basic essentials such as food, to higher order needs such as career development. Such subordination resulted in feelings of anger and powerlessness amongst athletes. Although identification was developed partly by the manipulation of symbols such as the 'signing on' ceremony, compliance was not entirely moral. For instance, team members, 'Undoubtedly saw instrumental value in giving their loyalty to such a powerful superordinate,' (p.405). Further, institutional factors such as the transfer rules created 'side bets,' (Becker, 1960), by making leaving difficult and expensive.

Coercion too played a part. Team members were continuously exhorted to remember their status as team members and not become involved in fights or be seen drinking beers. Individuals could also expect periodic public humiliation as the coach denigrated their performance in front of the whole team.

Loyalty was by no means universal. The authors suggest that the strongest bonds are forged where teams can develop all five components. They further suggest that individuals who are pre-disposed to the forgoing criteria will develop a more intense loyalty. Players not disposed to be loyal never became loyal. Moreover, their presence was damaging as it caused jealousy and mis-trust.

The existence of an element of calculative control does not by itself contradict Etzioni's theory. This is because Etzioni states that archetypal organizations tend to rely heavily but not necessarily exclusively upon a particular form of power. What is more important (and unclear), is the extent to which compliance was calculative.

Adler and Adler's study yields insight into the resource implications of creating intense loyalty. It is clearly an expensive process requiring intense and prolonged effort. This may explain why utilitarian organizations rarely succeed in acquiring cultural control. Quite apart from the fact that their 'for profit' motive is inconsistent with an appeal to values, (Drummond and Chell, 1992), it is impractical for most utilitarian organizations to concentrate resources in this way. This suggests that manipulating 'you ought to sentiments' (Ray, 1986) after the manner suggested by the 'excellence' school is an insufficient basis for generating commitment.

Asad's (1987) study of discipline in medieval monasteries explored how the 'will to obey,' (p.159) is created. The starting point for conversion is the idea that obedience is a virtue, something to be strived for. Humility is fundamental to conversion. Humility is achieved by a set of disciplinary practices, 'Aimed to construct and reorganise distinctive emotions,' (p.166). Disciplinary practices specify what is to be done, when and by whom. Unlike a prison, however, the monks are not restrained by physical ties but by fear of God. Seclusion is intended not to compel submission, but, to facilitate the exercise of virtue. The basis of discipline then, is not domination by an individual or regime, but authority. Obedience is due not to an individual but to the divinity. According to the divinity sin

55

endangers the soul and must therefore be continuously resisted. Within the monastery the abbot's authority is absolute. It is the abbot's duty to prescribe the steps towards the attainment of virtue. Since the abbot is Christ's representative, in obeying the abbot the monk obeys God's will.

Asad's analysis is based upon Benedictine and Cistercian rules. It is unclear how these were applied and experienced in practice. According to Asad, obedience was not always perfect. Monks occasionally fled from one monastery to another in order to escape from their abbot. Sometimes conflict between abbots and monks resulted in violence including murder. Such incidents were probably relatively rare. What is lacking, is detailed information about under what conditions authority collapsed. Even more interesting would be to know precisely what 'the will obey' meant to those seeking to observe it day in, day out.

Comparisons of compliance structures between extreme and mild coercive organizations

Etzioni hypothesises that alienation increases as coercion intensifies. Inmates in mildly coercive organizations such as detention centres and open prisons argues Etzioni, are less coerced and correspondingly less alienated than those incarcerated in extreme establishments such as maximum security jails.

Part of the evidence appears to refute this hypothesis. The exception is Bigelow and Driscoll's (1973) study of compliance relationships in a federal correction centre. This showed that inmates in strictly controlled dormitories subject to tighter, more coercive supervision, displayed less co-operative attitudes than those allowed access to workshops of the same institution where the atmosphere was more relaxed.

Conversely Smith and Hepburn (1977) found that alienation

was actually higher in both minimum and maximum security prisons than in medium security jails, and Alpert (1978), observed similar levels of alienation between inmates in medium and maximum security jails. All authors suggest similar explanations for their findings. Compliance theory, they argue, states that control rests on physical sanctions, it does not address the issue of confinement which is an alienating experience, regardless of the security designation. Smith and Hepburn (1977, p.258) attribute alienation in open prisons to 'The paradox of unrestrained freedom within broadly defined boundaries, and the simultaneous feeling of confinement'. Whereas in maximum security establishments, alienation results from absolute deprivation within a rigidly structured environment, in open prisons, coercion may be more subtle but not less alienating, especially when it is combined with vague, ambiguous rules. Alpert noted that lack of structure in open prisons conferred enormous informal power on prison staff which they used to punish inmates in an arbitrary manner. Consequently inmates came to view sanctions as unrelated to their behaviour, and hence beyond their control. The resultant feeling of powerlessness led to high levels of alienation.

These studies relate to an important element of Etzioni's theory as far as the present study is concerned. It is difficult however to be conclusive as there are only three of them and their findings conflict. Perhaps the most important point is that none have actually measured coercion and therefore they are only partial tests. It would have been very interesting to know whether inmates in maximum security jails perceived themselves as more coerced than those in open prisons, as the hypothesis of concomitant relations between power and involvement forms the basis of Etzioni's theory.

It is significant that illegitimate use of coercion is cited as particularly alienating, Etzioni suggests that this form of power is more damaging than legitimate coercion (Etzioni, 1968c). Moreover there is evidence to suggest that arbitrary use of punishment has a similar effect upon employees. (See Chapter Four).

Interesting too is the link between powerlessness and alienation identified by Alpert. Etzioni focuses upon the power of the organization as distinct from lower participant power. Yet there may be a link between the level of lower participant power and Etzioni's three forms of organization. Inmates in coercive organizations have least control over their lives. Employees in utilitarian organizations enjoy some control. Members of normative organizations may enjoy still more control though in the more extreme examples feelings of empowerment may be illusory as they reflect internalised acceptance of organizational dictates.

Partial tests of Etzioni's theory

Relationship between coercion and alienation in coercive organizations

There are numerous examples of evidence of a relationship between coercion and alienation in coercive organizations (e.g.; Thomas and Zingraff, 1976; Thomas, Kreps and Cage, 1977; Winfree and Woolf 1980) though correlations tend to be weak ranging 0.20 to 0.28. This has led researchers to examine the impact of inmates' social background and other factors upon involvement. For example, there is evidence to suggest that alienation intensifies as time goes on (Hyman, 1977; Larson, 1983); and, that it is lower amongst women who make friends in prison than those who remain isolated (Larson and Nelson 1984). Overall it appears that alienation is highest amongst those who experience strong feelings of powerlessness in prison and, who perceive their future life chances as negative (Thomas, 1975; Thomas, Petersen and Zingraff, 1978).

Interestingly, the evidence concerning inmate alienation in concentration camps suggests that far from resulting in intense hostility, exposure to extreme coercion brings about apathy (Bettleheim, 1943; Bloch,1947). Prolonged exposure to coercion may lead to devotion to the oppressors and readiness to identify with them. Hostility is deflected onto scapegoats, usually newcomers and low status prisoners (Cohen, 1953).

Coercion and alienation in utilitarian organizations

Although Etzioni says little about the role of negative sanctions in utilitarian organizations, there seems little doubt as to their existence. For example, Levinson (1973), and Moor and Wood (1979), have observed that chief executives often overlook the power of compliments and other forms of positive reinforcement in favour of nagging and threats to motivate senior managers. Similarly Likert (1958) suggests that closeness of supervision causes alienation especially amongst white collar workers.
 Knights and Roberts (1982) demonstrated the alienating effects of mental coercion in their study of the sales departments of four companies. Their research, which employed mainly in depth interviews, revealed how a 'Theory X' approach to management (McGregor, 1960), led to a spiral of coercion and alienation. Power was used to obtain commitment to sales targets by force. This instrumental attitude was reciprocated by staff's general discontent, insecurity and mental withdrawal from the work situation. Management responded by applying more coercion through threats, public humiliation and still tighter control via training, targets and competition. This resulted in high turnover. In one instance, those who could not leave adopted a counter coercive strategy by forming a union which then refused to accept management's methods of control. An attempt by one company to introducing special recognition for high performance failed because of fear of failure on the part of the staff, who distanced themselves further. Use of remunerative power by promises of rewards and promotion also failed because these never materialised, thus adding to the growing

sense of alienation. Otherwise withdrawal was the norm at all levels, so much so that the authors conclusions read almost like a study of inmates in concentration camp, 'Feeling unable to control or influence what is demanded of them for the sake of the company, they attempt to control all that is left - their own actions and attitudes,' (Knights and Roberts, 1982, p.61).

Although Etzioni links only physical sanctions with alienative involvement, this study shows that certain forms of control (e.g.; setting of targets, close supervision and humiliation of employees) are experienced as coercion and result in withdrawal -something which warrants investigation.

Compliance theory and effectiveness in coercive organizations

Etzioni argues that force is essential for containment yet much of the empirical evidence suggests that congruent compliance structures may actually be ineffective in coercive organizations. Glaser (1966) concluded that one reason for this is that prison staff create instability by suppressing activities perceived as potentially disruptive, and so deprive inmates of any legitimate means of relieving the strains and tensions of prison life.

Indeed there is evidence to suggest that prison guards find coercive tactics ineffective. This is partly because prison reforms have restricted their availability, and partly because formal sanctions are not invariably viewed by inmates as punishment. Coercion was viewed as potentially dangerous especially when dealing inmates who are depressed and lonely (Hepburn, 1985; Stojkovik, 1986). Stojkovik found that control relied on information provided by 'snitches' for rewards. This form of power was never officially acknowledged, but was considered vital in maintaining order amongst a hostile population. Interestingly Stojkovic suggested that stability probably rests upon the interaction between officer and inmate power. This idea has yet to be explored.

Even totalitarian regimes cannot impose their will completely.

Lammer's (1988) study of the Nazi occupation of Belgium illuminates the role of agency in power relations. According to Lammers 'Control agents can be influenced or even turned around by the organizations they are supposed to control,' (p. 442). For instance, the agent is obliged to rely upon the subordinate organization for information. The subordinate organization can impede the agent by implementing delaying tactics and protracted argument over petty details. Consequently the agent becomes an advocate for the subordinate organization pleading with headquarters for more time, leniency, relaxation of controls and so on.

Glaser (1966) also noted that the application of symbolic power in coercive settings generated stability. Far from being scorned, it was actually associated with successful rehabilitation. Officers exhibiting personal interest and encouragement towards inmates were equated with liking, stability and progress. Officials carrying out routine counselling within set procedures were ineffective.

On the whole though, it appears that containment and rehabilitation are hard to achieve. Thomas and Poole (1975) reviewing the evidence concluded that the two goals are incompatible such is the hostility aroused by coercion. Yet Jimmy Boyle's (1973) popular account of his prison experiences suggests that symbolic power may be effective even when inmates have become extremely alienated. Boyle describes how his increased defiance was followed by increased coercion until the authorities could no longer contain him. Boyle was therefore transferred, literally from a cage to a special unit utilising symbolic power. On arrival, he was immediately offered a cup of coffee by a warder and handed a knife to cut the string round his luggage. This marked the beginning of Boyle's subsequent rehabilitation.

The problem with most of this literature is that it views control of coercive organizations from the standpoint of the guards rather than the inmates. Whereas the guards may not perceive coercion as effective, this does not necessarily mean that inmates do not feel coerced. Moreover, these studies concentrate upon tactics, they say very little about the underlying structural power. Therefore although they may be viewed as potentially qualifying Etzioni's theory, they do not actually contradict it.

Compliance structures and effectiveness in normative organizations

Etzioni argues that organizations require compliance structures consistent with their goals if they are to be effective. The effects of a change from normative to utilitarian compliance structures were studied by Attewell and Gernstein (1979). The organization was a state controlled treatment centre for heroin addicts. Staff had no coercive control over patients, no means of remuneration, whilst normative rewards were made impossible by the degrading nature of the treatment. Expulsion was unavailable as it was against medical ethics. Compliance therefore came to depend on the loyalty between staff and patients generated by daily interaction. The programme was government funded and became subject to increased formal control. Staff became subject to growing surveillance and their role changed from providing support and help, to urine monitors and rule enforcers. This led to role conflict on their part whilst the clients became alienated and left. Consequently the programme failed.

Fourcher's (1975) account of the effect of a change of mental health service organizations from custodial 'mental institutions' to preventative community based services, showed how staff could frustrate change instead of becoming victims of it. Fourcher describes how these theoretically normative organizations, were in fact composed of sufficiently large numbers of non-professional staff to tilt the organizations towards a predominantly utilitarian orientation. The non-professionals successfully impeded progress by pressing bureaucratic issues over policy, which diverted the energy of professionals into utilitarian concerns over funding and resources, and away from implementing policy change. The obstructors succeeded because the organization's decision-making structures had not been amended to take account of the new normative orientation.

A mixed compliance structure can also inhibit an organization from achieving its goals. Mulford (1978) attributed the failure of certain public policies to incongruent compliance structures. Policies were conceived by top level administrators and tended to reflect their normative, idealistic orientation. Implementation however was at the hands of lower ranking non-professional staff who were not interested in ideals. So, by executing normative policies in a utilitarian fashion, the policy maker's aims were sabotaged.

Kieser's (1987; 1989) studies of monasticism and medieval craft guilds respectively shows how incongruence may destroy organizations. Paradoxically the monk's renunciation of wealth resulted in monasteries becoming extremely wealthy. Possession of wealth corrupted religious asceticism leading to the downfall of monastic foundations. Medieval craft guilds were protectionist organizations. Their monopolistic powers and normative functions of providing social support to members restricted the guilds' ability to respond to the early industrial revolution. Consequently, the guilds were circumnavigated in favour of the new factories and subsequently dis-integrated.

An interesting example of how organizations seek to maintain congruence is contained in Burn's, Andersen and Shortell's (1990) comparison of control strategies between public and private (for profit) hospitals. Whereas one would expect the latter to exhibit a lower level of normative control and a higher level of remunerative control than the former, the opposite proved to be the case. Private hospitals deliberately placed physicians on the board of directors and avoided making them dependent on the hospital for their salary in order to avoid any appearance of immorality emanating from their 'for profit' orientation. Such management was reflected in higher levels of physician satisfaction in private hospitals.

63

Although normative organizations require comparatively little control because of members' pre-disposition to high involvement, all organizations must possess some means of integrating members' energies and enthusiasm with organizational goals. Oliver (1989) explored the problem of reconciling control and ideology in a small cooperative dealing in bicycles. Control was basically normative resting upon a tacit negotiated code of conduct. Unwritten rules were supplemented by bureaucratic control. A major part of the function of bureaucracy was to prevent resources being consumed in endless meetings over operational and administrative details leading Oliver to suggest that such organizations require more rather than less instrumental control even though total membership of the collective never exceeded seven.

Interesting though these studies are, they are really about applying Etzioni's theory to interpret the consequences of change. In so doing, they demonstrate its usefulness in understanding behaviour in organizations. They do not however constitute evidence of the theory's validity for as Hall, Haas and Johnson (1967) observed, an organization's title is a poor guide to its compliance structure which needs to be established empirically.

For instance, Murphy (1980) demonstrated how appearance of symbolic power can be used to mask coercion. His study of an African tribe showed how elders used secret symbolic power to control youthful members of the tribe. Secrets, symbolised in snakes, thunder and medicines were guarded jealously, and used as a distancing mechanism between elders and youths. These secret powers provided a mystical legitimation, and a scared veil beneath which, elders could control the youths and manipulate the community. Likewise, Katz's (1982) analysis of the implementation of the Nazi Holocaust showed how officers working within an ostensibly normative hierarchy appealing to honour and pride, exploited their discretionary powers to kill in the hope of advancing their careers. Thus although the Nazi organization might have been a normative structure (albeit an unusual one), the involvement of its officials was predominantly calculative.

Conclusions

The main point emerging from this review is that Etzioni's theory is virtually unresearched, especially the core propositions pertaining to relationships between power and involvement between the three types of organization. The most that can be said about the preceding studies is that they provide some very tenuous evidence to support Etzioni's theory. Even this watery conclusion is subject to numerous qualifications. No study directly compares power and involvement in all three types of organization using validated measures. Such comparisons as do exist are based on a comparatively narrow range of organizations and most studies confine themselves to only one kind of organization. Consequently those studies which appear to contradict Etzioni may be more the product of their methodology than any weakness in Etzioni's theory. The same criticism applies to findings which support the theory. At best they are partial tests; at worst, the use of unvalidated measures and only vaguely relevant operationalisations of constructs, renders their conclusions questionable.

This review has concentrated mainly upon sociological research concerning to compliance variables. Psychologists have researched the relationship between leader reward and punishment behaviour and employee satisfaction, and also attempted to identify the correlates of organizational commitment a construct which closely resembles Etzioni's concept of involvement. These studies are examined in the next two chapters.

4 The psychological literature on compliance in organizations

Introduction

Psychologists have been less concerned with power in organizations as such than with examining the impact of persuasive and coercive behaviours on various groups of employees. Most of the work is empirical, there has been comparatively little theorizing. Studies can be classified into two main areas of interest (Kipnis, Schmidit and Wilkinson, 1980):

1 How people influence colleagues to obtain benefits or satisfy organizational goals.

2 How subordinates can be influenced to improve morale and productivity.

This chapter includes studies pertaining to both areas though the emphasis is on the latter. This is because it relates to supervisor/subordinate relations and the impact of rewards and punishments on various forms of employee satisfaction, variables analogous to power and involvement.

Etzioni suggests that rewards and punishments are positively and negatively related to involvement respectively. This is a commonly held view; for example, Raven and Kruglanski (1970) suggest that coercion creates conflict, rejection and the desire to retaliate. Once coercion has been applied, influence tactics are usually avoided. Similarly, Luthans and Kreitner (1985) note that punishment appears to be less effective in modifying behaviour than reward. Punishment, they suggest, merely results in temporary cessation of undesirable behaviour. Moreover, punishment has un-predictable and destructive side effects. It may cause emotional and anxious responses including an immutable dislike towards the person administering sanctions and permanent suppression of desirable behaviours. Although Luthans and Kreitner argue that punishment should therefore be avoided, it will become clear later in this chapter that the empirical evidence is divided. Punishment may have beneficial as well as adverse consequences. Indeed, it may be essential to the management of the organization as a whole.

Conversely, rewards are generally believed to result in satisfaction and liking. Although research broadly supports this idea, as far as recipients are concerned, the impact upon bystanders is less predictable.

Factors influencing selection of power tactic and the use of power

It was emphasised in Chapter One that Etzioni views power as a structural phenomenon though it was argued that in reality, power emanates from many sources and it may not always be possible for powerholders to mobilise their formal powers (e.g., dismissal may be constrained by law). Studies reviewed in this section examine the nature of power tactics used in various situations.

Miller, Bosler, Rollof and Seibold (1977) studied choice of power tactics in situations where power holders had no formal authority whatsoever. Overall, they found a preference for 'friendly persuasion'. In interpersonal situations, use of threats was unlikely, whilst in non-interpersonal contexts expertise, (defined as mobilization of logical argument) was the most favoured tactic followed by reward.

Kipnis, Schmidit and Wilkinson (1980) studied selection of influence tactics in a variety of hypothetical situations. A group of postgraduate business studies students employed in mainly managerial roles, were asked to describe an incident of how they got what they wanted from their superior, a co-worker and a subordinate. Responses suggested that choice of tactic was determined by three factors: what the respondents were trying to get; the amount of resistance shown, and the power of the target person. Sanctions and negative actions tended to be used where a target was resisting actively or where the reasons for the request related to a respondent's role in the organization. The important point about this study was that the range and type of tactics revealed bore no resemblance to theoretical models such as those of Etzioni and French and Raven. These make no mention of deception and clandestine moves, just two of the tactics revealed. Kipnis et al. concluded that people in organizations do not always exert influence in neat and readily classifiable ways. They also pointed out that whereas most organizational texts are concerned with downward power, their study demonstrated that power in organizations is multi-directional - everyone is influencing everyone else.

Beyer and Trice (1984) subsequently qualified these findings. They report that possession of power stimulates managers to use discipline especially where company policy encourages it. In other words, structure reinforces the use of power. This does not mean power is applied impartially. Beyer and Trice found older employees tended to be dealt with more gently by suspension on leave instead of dismissal and that women tended to be treated more chivalrously. There is also evidence to support Etzioni's theory that senior managers are less coerced, (Beyer and Trice 1984; Trice and Beyer 1977; Rosen and Jerdee

1974). These studies report that professionals and managers generally received fewer warnings than those lower down the hierarchy and were more likely to escape punishment for specific instances of misconduct.

Supervisor's use of rewards and punishments

Studies reviewed here examine the relationship between supervisors' use of rewards and punishments, and constructs of employee satisfaction. Researchers have tended to operationalise reward and punishment on four dimensions:

1   *Contingency reward* - rewards given in response to good behaviour and performance.

2   *Non-contingency reward* - rewards which are unrelated to behaviour or performance.

3   *Contingency punishment* - the imposition of sanctions in response to poor performance or inappropriate behaviour.

4   *Non-contingency punishment* - the imposition of sanctions which are unrelated to performance or behaviour, e.g., blaming an employee for something he has no control over.

Most of the scales used in the literature and the present study (see Chapter Eight), are versions of a questionnaire developed by Johnson (1973). Consequently there is some consistency between studies.

Intuitively one might think that reward results in satisfaction and high performance and punishment results in dis-satisfaction and poor performance. The evidence, however, suggests that the relationship between these variables is by no means as clear and simple.

Sims and Syzalgyi (1975) examined the relationship between contingency reward and contingency punishment behaviours and subordinate satisfaction and performance across four groups of hospital staff; administrative, professional, technical and service. Strong positive correlations between positive reward behaviour and satisfaction were observed, particularly in relation to satisfaction with supervision. Correlations between punitive behaviour and satisfaction were negative but mainly insignificant.

The administrative group were an exception, satisfaction and punishment being positively related. A secondary analysis based on role ambiguity showed positive correlations were higher for staff whose roles were unclear. It was concluded that where staff are uncertain about their roles, any form of direction, positive or negative helps reduce ambiguity and thereby contributes to satisfaction.

Arvey, Davis and Nelson (1984) also recorded positive correlations between punishment behaviour and satisfaction with supervision though these were substantially weaker than correlations between rewards and satisfaction. Likewise Podsakoff and Todor (1985) found both contingency reward and contingency punishment were positively related to group drive, cohesiveness and productivity. Non-contingency rewards and punishments were negatively related. Weak positive relations between coercive behaviours and satisfaction have also been noted by Reitz (1971) and Gaski (1984).

71

Weak negative and negligible correlations between measures of satisfaction and punishment have also been recorded. Podsakoff, Todor and Skov (1982) found positive relationships between contingency reward and performance, satisfaction with supervision, and promotion opportunities especially amongst high performers. Contingency punishment had little effect on performance or any measure of satisfaction. Non-contingency punishment was equally dissatisfying to both low and high performers.

This study was based solely on a group of medical personnel. It was followed by more extensive survey in local government, hospital and state departments sampling a wide range of staff, including professionals and blue collar workers (Podsakoff, Todor, Gorver and Huber 1984). Contingency reward behaviour had the strongest relationship with performance and satisfaction, followed by non-contingent reward behaviour. Relationships between contingency punishment and non-contingency punishment, and performance and satisfaction, were either weak or negligible.

Not surprisingly, Arvey and Jones's (1985) in their review of the literature on the effect of punishment on job satisfaction and performance, were unable to detect any consistency between results. They could only note that studies have suggested no relationship, as well as positive and negative effects. They suggested this could be a reflection of research methodology, in particular failure to take account of factors such as organization level and the differential effects of punishment on high and low performers. They also argued that contingency punishment could be perceived as a sign of good management - 'firm but fair.' This implies that where punishment is administered contingently, it does not automatically result in hostility and alienation. Indeed, working in such a climate may add to satisfaction.

The inconsistent findings concerning punishment have yet to be resolved. For instance, Stepina et al. (1991) found that only contingent reward was related to satisfaction with supervision. Other forms of reward and punishment appeared to have no influence whatever.

Although the relationship between contingent reward and satisfaction appears to be positive, there is evidence to suggest that satisfaction with supervision is partly a function of the degree of congruence between employees' preferred form of inducements and reported forms of influence (Vechio and Sussmann, 1989).

The relationship between reward behaviours and performance is likewise generally positive. Korukonda and Hunt (1989), however, argue that these results may reflect a self-fulfilling prophesy. That is, a subordinate who is dis-satisfied with the leader may report that the leader engages in non-contingent punishment behaviours. Since it is the same subordinate who reports on satisfaction with the leader, 'It is questionable whether the established relationship between the independent and criterion variables represents the true impact of the leader's reward/punishment behaviour,' (p.307). Korukonda and Hunt further argue that previous studies may suffer from attribution bias first by asking the leader to rate subordinates' performance, and second because individuals may ascribe success to their own efforts and abilities and failure to the organization. Consequently rewards may be inevitably perceived as contingent and punishment inevitably perceived as non-contingent. Korukonda and Hunt therefore adopted an experimental approach whereby performance was measured by the number of cards correctly sorted by respondents. Reward and punishment were based on points allocation.

Both contingent and non-contingent reward resulted in positive perceptions of the leader whereas non-contingent punishment resulted in the opposite. Moreover the reactions to non-contingency punishment were highly variable thus supporting Luthans and Kreitner's (1985) assertion concerning the arbitrary effects of punishment. Contrary to previous studies, performance was unaffected by contingent reward whereas contingent punishment positively benefited it.

Korukonda and Hunt suggest that the stimulus to productivity is that contingency punishment implies disapproval whereas reward signifies approval of current performance. Yet as Korukonda and Hunt acknowledge, the effect may be salutary as long term performance could not be measured.

The most consistent finding emerging from the literature is the depressing effect of non-contingency punishment upon satisfaction. Arbitrary behaviour by supervisors may create feelings of powerlessness, that is, 'Perhaps when discipline is non-contingent, employees turn to other mechanisms to escape, avoid or gain retribution. It may be exactly these kind of conditions which produce frustration, apathy, sabotage and theft,' (Arvey and Jones, 1985, p.390).

Impact of rewards and punishments upon bystanders

Rewards and punishments are not administered in isolation. They may affect co-workers as well as recipients. Although it was noted earlier in this Chapter that Luthans and Kreitner (1985) urge organizations to avoid sanctions, this advice fails to take into account the feelings of bystanders. Ignoring misdemeanours and/or administering undeserved rewards may demoralise high performers who perceive themselves as implicitly punished (Schnake and Dumler, 1989). Conversely punishing miscreants tacitly rewards those whose conduct conforms to requirements. Moreover, contingency rewards and punishment not only reduce ambiguity for recipients, they enable everyone to understand what constitutes desirable and undesirable behaviour.

Some empirical support exists for these arguments. O'Reilly and Puffer (1989) observed that contingent reward enhanced bystander's expressed, (as distinct from observed), motivation, productivity and perceived equity. Failure to administer sanctions depressed all of these factors. There was some evidence to suggest that reward had more impact than punishment. Significantly, ignoring poor performance had the most detrimental effect upon satisfaction.

Influence of subordinate on selection of power tactic

Etzioni argues that organizations base their compliance structures on participant's motivation to comply which may be hostile, calculative or moral. Research supports this hypothesis in as much as it reveals that a supervisor's propensity to reward or punish is determined by their perceptions of employees' performance and attitude to work. It is not known whether it is the attitude of the supervisor or the behaviour of the employee which initiates the process of interaction.

The intuitive view is that the supervisor's attitude is critical to productivity. Blau and Scott (1963), however, suggest it could be the opposite, that is, the attitude of a supervisor may actually be the result of a group's low productivity. Faced with a hostile or indifferent group, supervisors may adopt a more coercive attitude than they would with an enthusiastic one. There is some empirical support for this. Kipnis' (1976) study of business and navy departments found that supervisors responded systematically to employee performance. Where incompetence was diagnosed, supervisors tended to apply expert power. Where poor performance was attributed to idleness or poor attitude, supervisors tended to resort to multiple means of influence with emphasis upon coercion.

Sims (1980) also noted that both longitudinal and laboratory studies show that punishment is more the result of employee behaviour than the cause. Managers tend to respond more positively when dissatisfied with performance than when dissatisfied with an employee's attitude.

Chow and Grusky (1980) in an experimental study tested the hypothesis that workers' performance and behaviour causes supervisory style rather than the reverse. The results showed that low productivity led to closer supervision, though not in the case of aggressive employees, where supervisors preferred to avoid contact and resort to punitive responses.

Subsequently, Zahn and Wolf (1981) suggested that the relationship is reciprocal in that both leader and subordinates provide stimuli to one another, and that the relationship between them is predictable from their early exchanges. Interestingly, they argue that since this means that the relationship between a manager and his subordinates is interdependent it is futile to think of a manager as having a particular style.

These studies seem to have prompted a change in emphasis. Arvey (1980) said that research needed to determine how punishment can be used to accomplish behaviourial change. Podsakoff (1982) argued this approach is partial. Most early studies he said, were based on a belief that supervisors lead and subordinates followed. Hence it was assumed that it was more important to understand supervisors' ability to change the subordinate, than vice versa. However as results had demonstrated that supervisor/subordinate relationships are reciprocal, then logically, subordinate behaviour could cause changes in leadership style.

Reviewing the evidence, Podsakoff (1982) observed that although research was in its infancy it was apparent that the most significant determinant of punishment is employee performance. Supervisors tend to be more punishing where this was attributable to poor attitude rather than to ineptness. Less experienced and less confident supervisors relied more on punishments. Also, supervisors of large workforces spent less time coaxing problem workers and were therefore more likely to use punishments. No other variables (e.g., task structure and complexity, nature of leader's reinforcement power, effects of matrix organization and ingratiating behaviour) were consistently related to punishment.

Accordingly, subsequent research has concentrated upon performance. Sims and Manz (1984) found verbal reward behaviour was positively related to performance. Punitive statements were higher where performance was low. Supervisor's personal circumstances affect their responses to employees. Tjosvold (1985a, 1985b) found competitive supervisors were more intolerant of poor performers than co-operative ones. Both competitive and co-operative supervisors however, resorted to threats, and came to dislike subordinates whose poor performance was attributed to inadequate motivation.

A supervisor's evaluation of employee performance may affect factors besides punishment. Greene (1972) found compliance (defined as frequency of carrying out tasks required by the supervisor) related strongly to job satisfaction and also role accuracy. In turn both compliance and role accuracy were lower where the supervisor's evaluation of subordinates' performance was low.

Effects of restricting power

Ng (1980) has asked, if power corrupts does powerlessness also corrupt? Kanter (1979) has suggested it tends to breed 'bossiness' in managers rather than true leadership. Likewise, Drummond (1991) has argued that managers who feel powerless are more likely to behave in arbitrary and underhand manner those who perceive themselves as in command. This view is supported empirically in that Greene and Podsakoff (1981) operationalised French and Raven's typology to test the effects of withdrawing supervisors' reward power. The result was a substantial increase in the use of punishment but not greater recourse to expert or referent power. There were indications that increased punishment would ultimately lead to dissatisfaction, absenteeism and high turnover.

Does power alienate power holders?

Etzioni's theory focuses upon the effects of power on power subjects. Kipnis (1972) has suggested, however, that possession of power tends to alienate those who wield it. This is because power fundamentally concerns the ability to determine the behaviour of others. People in possession of this capability view power subjects as alien objects of manipulation and become increasingly psychologically distant from them. Consequently power holders tend to devalue the performance of the power subject.

The interesting point about this is it suggests alienation is reciprocal and determined by the level of control. In coercive organizations, the power of guards is almost absolute compared with that of powerholder's in utilitarian and normative organizations. Does this mean they are correspondingly more alienated from the power subjects?

Discussion and conclusions

The studies reviewed in this chapter ostensibly dispose of Etzioni's theory. Not only do they show that power holders utilize a far wider repertoire than Etzioni's three forms of power, but that if in organizations everyone is influencing everyone else, then how can power be regarded as a structural phenomenon?

Studies reviewed here, however, are concerned more with forms of power or tactics than power bases or resources. Etzioni's theory is concerned with the latter. Even so, the potential impact of coercive tactics on involvement cannot be ignored. Perhaps the most significant thing to emerge from

78

these studies is that they clearly demonstrate the existence of mental coercion within organizations. Although the results do not altogether support the idea of a negative relationship between coercion and satisfaction, there have been comparatively few studies and results are by no means unequivocal. It should also be borne in mind that these studies were undertaken in employing organizations primarily amongst white collar and professional staff. The level of coercion could well have been quite low. Further, these results are inconsistent with those sociological studies (e.g., Knights and Roberts, 1982) which indicate a negative relationship between coercion and involvement related constructs.

One possible explanation for this inconsistency is that contingency reward and contingency punishment measure the same phenomenon, one from a positive angle, the other from a negative one. That is, both are ultimately based in the organization's power to hire, fire and promote. Yet if this were so, why are the results for punishment inconsistent; and why is it less strongly related to satisfaction? It is also apparent that non-contingency punishment has a negative impact on satisfaction. The implications of this for the development of the research model and measurement of the study variables are discussed in Chapters Six and Eight.

It could be argued that these findings are inconsequential as Etzioni defined coercion physically, whereas here it has been operationalised psychologically as 'an aversive or noxious consequence' (Sims and Szilagyi, 1975, p.428). Yet surely physical sanctions are aversive and noxious? Further, is it realistic to conceive coercion in purely physical terms? It seems highly improbable that stripping someone of freedom, rights and possessions does not inflict mental, as well as physical damage.

The multi-directional nature of influence might also be seen to obviate the idea that power in organizations is structural and predominantly downwards. The key word here however is influence. There is no agreement amongst theorists as to whether influence is or is not a form of power. Some have argued that because influence is a means of getting someone to do what he might otherwise have not, it is a form of power. Others have maintained that unlike power, influence ultimately lacks the ability to compel. It is a means of restructuring a person's perception. A person can refuse to yield to influence but not to power (Wrong, 1979). The work of Kipnis et al. (1980) tested situations which included those where respondents had no hierarchial power, therefore whilst it seems plausible that in organizations everyone is attempting to influence everyone else, only persons in power positions have the resources to substantiate influence.

Greene and Podsakoff's study of the effects of withdrawing reward power showed that the use of referent power also declined, suggesting the two may be interdependent. A study by Ornstein (1986) on the relationship between organizational symbols and perceived organizational climate found that reward and empathic symbols tended to be processed together. Since referent power and empathic symbols closely resemble normative power, this suggests that financial and symbolic rewards are used considerably more in concert than Etzioni's theory would suggest.

Finally it is interesting to note that there is evidence which consistently links rewards and satisfaction. This accords with Etzioni's theory on positive relations between symbolic and remunerative forms of power and involvement. However, none of the studies reviewed in this chapter directly operationalise Etzioni's concepts and therefore the evidence should not be regarded as conclusive in this respect.

5 Organization commitment

Introduction

The theoretical discussion in Chapter Three established that involvement may be viewed as a process whereby individuals come to think about and evaluate their position in an organization (Kanter, 1968). It was seen as consisting of a combination of attitudinal and behaviourial elements. Involvement, it was noted, has a distinct organizational focus though it is related to other constructs notably work alienation, job satisfaction and Central Life Interest. There are many definitions and measures of organizational involvement. In the psychological literature it is known as commitment and is generally regarded as comprising loyalty, willingness to exert effort and, acceptance of organizational goals and values.

The concept of commitment corresponds closely with Etzioni's concept of involvement. The purpose of this Chapter is to examine the commitment literature as it shows that involvement or commitment may be affected by many other variables besides power. Since the number of studies is vast this discussion is extremely selective. For comprehensive reviews see Mowday, Porter and Steers (1982) and Mathieu and Zajac (1990).

Figure Two summarises how researchers have approached organization commitment topic. The various studies have been

81

concerned with identifying its antecedents, correlates and consequences. Each of these is considered below.

ORGANIZATION COMMITMENT		
ANTECEDENTS	CORRELATES	CONSEQUENCES
Personal characteristics	Motivation	Withdrawal behaviours
Role status	Job involvement	Job performance
Job characteristics	Stress	
Group/leader relations	Occupational	
Organizational	commitment	
characteristics	Union commitment	
	Job satisfaction	

Figure 2 Classification of antecedents, correlates and consequences of organizational commitment

(Adapted from Mathieu and Zajac, 1990)

Antecedents of organizational commitment

Personal characteristics

Commitment is positively associated with age and tenure (Mowday, Porter and Steers, 1982). Age appears to be more strongly related to attitudinal than calculative forms of commitment (Mathieu and Zajac, 1990). It is unclear why this is so. One possibility is that so called 'side bets' (Becker, 1960) may not exert such a powerful influence upon employees after all. That is, employees remain because they want to rather than because they are trapped by accumulated investments such as pensions and other service benefits. Another possibility is that attitudinal commitment merely reflects individuals' need for self justification. Having remained with the organization for so long, individuals need to persuade themselves the decision is one of choice rather than force of circumstances. Another possible explanation is that the privileges of seniority result in a benign attitude towards the organization (Mathieu and Zajac, 1990). It seems reasonable to suggest that these explanations are partial. Tenure probably reflects a combination of varying degrees calculation, self-justification and affective emotions.

Education is inversely and weakly related to commitment. The suggested explanation is that educated individuals have high career expectations which organizations are not always able to fulfil. Professionals may also be more committed to their occupational group than the organization. Commitment is gender related, being higher for women than men, and higher for married women than married men (Mowday et al., 1982; Mathieu and Zajac, 1990).

Central Life Interest and commitment correlate positively (Dubin, Champoux and Porter, 1975). A similar relationship exists between attitudinal (but not calculative) commitment and the Protestant work ethic (Kidron, 1978). The link between commitment and religion is unclear. Although there is evidence to suggest that a substantial proportion of decision makers in organizations rely upon divine guidance, Chusmir and Koberg's (1988) survey of managerial employees and non-managerial employees revealed no correlation between organizational commitment and religious affiliation (including Protestants, Catholics and Eastern religions), or depth of religious conviction.

Importance of the early employment period

The very early employment period is thought to be a critical determinant of subsequent commitment as this is a time when attitudes may undergo rapid change as the employee experiences the organization first hand. The evidence suggests that highly committed entrants are likely to remain so. However, disappointment with the organization most affects the highly committed (Brockner, Tyler and Cooper-Schneider, 1992).

Those leaving during the first fifteen months of employment tended to display a marked fall in commitment prior to departure. Otherwise commitment levels appear to stabilise beyond the first month or so of employment. Initial experiences may be influential for a long time however. Witt and Beorkem (1991) observed that employees experiencing severe role conflict tend to re-evaluate their commitment to the organization on the basis of their initial work assignments.

Organization dependability, feelings of personal importance to the organization, and fulfilment of expectations increase commitment. Awareness of positive attitudes towards the organization by co-workers also contributes to commitment. The same applies to perceived equity of pay, group norms of hard work, and social involvement in the organization (Mowday, et al., 1982).

Isolated studies indicate the existence of a correlation between need fulfilment and commitment. For example Hall, Schneider and Nygren (1970) studied the impact of personal factors on moral commitment, (defined as a process by which the goals of the organization and the individual merge and become congruous). Commitment was related to satisfaction of higher order needs and increased over time. Likewise, perceived competence correlates moderately and positively with attitudinal commitment (Mathieu and Zajac, 1990).

Role states and job characteristics

Mowday et al. conclude that situational factors have more impact on commitment than personal ones. Previous studies, they note, have consistently recorded positive relationships between commitment and job scope, and negative relationships between commitment and role conflict. Results on role ambiguity are mixed though there is strong and consistent evidence to suggest that role overload depresses commitment (Mathieu and Zajac, 1990).

Mid- and late- career involvement has received little attention. Buchanan's (1974) exploratory study is one of the few contributions in this area. His longitudinal analysis focused on the commitment of managers in mid- and late-career over a five year period. He found that initial job assignments, job achievement and hierarchical advancement positively affected its development. Similarly Cheeny (1983) found that organizational identification was strongly linked to participation in decision making and supervisory experience and inversely related to job mobility. Cheeny's study is interesting because it is one of the few to use interviews. The results appear to be broadly consistent with those obtained by Buchanan who used psychometric scales.

Volunteers have received little attention in the literature. Daily (1985) found that the key factors determining their commitment are similar to those affecting paid employees, namely job satisfaction, work autonomy, job involvement and feedback from the work itself.

Group/leader relations

Peer relations may have an important influence upon commitment. Vancouver and Schmidt (1991) observed that colleagues' commitment to organizational goals had a greater impact upon job attitudes including commitment than supervisor/subordinate congruence.

Organizational characteristics

Mowday et al. noted that, although commitment levels fluctuate from organization to organization, this phenomena has yet to be investigated. The same can be said for the relationship between hierarchical level and commitment. Clegg and Wall's (1981) study of British study of blue collar, supervisory and white collar professional staff found that commitment (and also job satisfaction) rose with organizational level.

Wall et al. (1986) investigated the long-term effects of the implementation of autonomous work groups on a number of variables including commitment. The research organization studied had changed from a traditional hierarchical structure, to one where group members became self-supervising with responsibility for allocating tasks and ensuring that targets were met. A flat managerial structure was introduced along with a single status canteen, single status car parking, abolition of time clocks and monthly payment by credit transfer. Although a substantial and sustained increase in intrinsic job satisfaction was observed, commitment was unaffected. The authors suggested autonomous work groups probably divert their commitment away from the organization onto the work group.

Investigations concerning the impact of culture on commitment have produced counter-intuitive results. Comparisons between American and Japanese workers show that commitment is lower amongst the latter (Luthans, McCaul Dodd, 1985; Near, 1989). Indeed the growing corpus of studies consistently indicates that the quality of working life in Japan is poor. Japanese workers appear to experience greater work place tension and lower levels of satisfaction than their Western counterparts (Drummond, 1992).

Correlates of organizational commitment

It was suggested in Chapter Two that need fulfilment and satisfaction are linked. The evidence broadly supports this idea and suggests that work involvement and related concepts such as motivation, occupational commitment, job involvement and job satisfaction correlate positively with commitment. Certain of these constructs appear to be more strongly related to attitudinal than calculative commitment (Mathieu an 1990).

Bateman and Strasser (1984) attempted to establis relationships between commitment, and both personal a... situational variables. Citing for example Marsh and Mannari (1977), and Price and Mueller (1981), they argued that researchers have tended to rely upon explanations derived from exchange theory to justify presumed causal linkages between satisfaction and commitment. An important feature of this study is that it is one of the few to have explored the relationship between commitment and rewards and punishment. This alone was an important contribution to research. Mowday et al. (1982) for instance could only speculate that high commitment would be associated with supervision that was not too tight or too close.

Bateman and Strasser used Porter and Smith's (1970) Organizational Commitment Questionnaire, the most commonly used measure of commitment in the literature. This operationalises involvement as willingness to stay; to exert effort and to remain loyal to the organization. Leader behaviours were measured using contingency reward and punishment scales originally developed by Johnson (1973). It was concluded that variables previously associated with commitment such as employment alternatives, job tension and need achievement were actually antecedent to job satisfaction, and that commitment is one cause of satisfaction. Of the twelve variables investigated, overall job satisfaction and employment alternatives accounted for most of the variance in organizational commitment.

The impact of rewards and punishments on commitment was negligible. Whilst this might indicate that Etzioni's theory is misconceived, it is important to bear in mind that Etzioni argues that rewards and punishment vary considerably between different types of organization. It is possible that more extreme levels of reward and punishment such as might apply in coercive or extreme normative organizations, would have more impact than 'medium' levels. Clearly more research is needed to confirm these results.

Bateman and Strasser were primarily concerned with the relationship between commitment and job satisfaction. Curry et al. (1986) utilised a similar design, model and sample but incorporated a wider range of controls than Bateman and Strasser. This showed that high levels of fairness of rewards were associated with high satisfaction and high commitment. Contrary to Bateman and Strasser's findings, their results provided no evidence that commitment has a causal effect on satisfaction. Moreover they could find no evidence in either direction for a causal effect between satisfaction and commitment. Curry et al. concluded that taken together, the two studies cast doubt over previous assumptions about the antecedents of both satisfaction and commitment.

Vandenberg and Lance (1992) concluded that commitment causes satisfaction though their study was based upon an unconventional measure of job satisfaction. Mathieu (1991) could only suggest that commitment and job satisfaction are related and that satisfaction may have more influence on commitment than the reverse. The precise nature of the relationship remains a mystery. Mathieu has speculated that the two variables may be dimensions of a more global construct. The nature of that construct, if it exists, has yet to be elucidated. Mathieu and Zajac (1990) suggest that commitment, job involvement, job satisfaction, motivation and so forth may reflect a more general emotional response to the work environment moderated, in part, by the extent to which the organization is able to provide satisfying work, opportunities for growth and so on.

One possibility is that the 'missing link' is power. Assuming power is structurally determined it exists then as a 'given' feature of the organization. If Etzioni's theory that power influences involvement is correct, then conceivably satisfaction and involvement and so forth are affective reactions to the organizational power structure.

Empirical support for this suggestion may be adduced from the literature. In Chapter Three the studies of coercive organizations clearly indicated that oppression is associated with dissatisfaction. Conversely, Kushman's (1992) study of teacher commitment both to the organization and to student learning. Kushman concluded that commitment to the school was a function of empowerment. Empowerment consisted of two dimensions. First, staffs' perceived efficacy which was related to control over the teaching process. Second, through membership of a powerful group. The latter arose through collaborative leadership, signified by joint goals, and joint problem solving. In other words, power was used not to restrain or to induce compliance, but, to create a framework for achievement. Consequently the school concerned was viewed by staff as a 'professionally rich and satisfying place of work,' (p 27).

Another possible explanation for the apparent lack of causal effects may be the tautological nature of items used to measure constructs of satisfaction and organization commitment. For instance, as Mathieu and Zajac (1990) note, the item 'I'll stay overtime to finish a job even if I'm not paid for it,' in Lodahl and Kejner's job involvement scale is similar to the item 'I am willing to put in a great deal of effort beyond that normally expected in order to help this organization be successful,' (p.183) in Porter and Smith's widely used Organization Commitment Scale.

Consequences of organization commitment

It has been suggested that organizations require the positive orientation of participants. Two main outcomes of commitment have been studied by researchers; withdrawal behaviours and performance. Studies show weak negative relationships between commitment and lateness and turnover and a weak positive relationship between commitment and attendance.

Correlations between commitment and turnover-related intentions are stronger (Mathieu and Zajac, 1990).

One consistent and counter-intuitive finding is that organizational commitment appears to have little effect upon performance (e.g.; Angle and Perry, 1981; Farrell and Rusbult, 1981, Bluedorn, 1982; Randell, 1990) Studies which have distinguished between attitudinal and calculative components of commitment have produced conflicting results. Meyer et al. (1989) observed that affective commitment was positively related to job performance whereas continuance commitment was negatively related. Johnston and Snizek (1991) however found that continuance commitment was positively related to performance, whereas the relationship with moral involvement was negative. Most recently Meyer and Schoorman (1992) observed that performance (based on analysis of performance appraisal schedules) was moderately and positively related to moral involvement whereas correlations between performance and continuance commitment were negligible and insignificant. Most important perhaps is the fact that none of these studies have found strong relationships between performance and any form of commitment.

Fisher (1980) has argued that basic assumption of a link between attitudes and behaviour is flawed. Indeed performance may be affected by variables beyond an employee's control - a point which is emphasised in the literature upon 'total quality management' (e.g., Deming, 1986)

Yet as Mowday et al. (1982) argue, it seems inconceivable that an individual's willingness to exert effort on behalf of the organization is not somehow reflected in performance. The most obvious explanation for the weak correlations is the arid manner in which performance is measured. Performance is potentially a multi-dimensional phenomenon consisting of efforts, care and attention and so forth. Constraining measurement within single item ratings by supervisors, performance appraisal data and experimental simulations of speed and

accuracy may result in more significant dimensions of p
ance eluding investigators.

Dimensions of organizational commitment

An important theoretical development in commitment research
has been the identification of different forms of commitment
which go beyond the basic distinction between attitudinal and
calculative components. Bar-Hayim and Berman (1992), for
example, have demonstrated that scales forumlated by Porter
and Smith (1970) and Cook and Wall (1980) factor into two
components entitled passive and active. The former equates to
desire to remain with the organization. The latter refers to
identification and involvement with the organization, that is,
feelings of belonging, willingness to exert effort for the organization and awareness that one's efforts benefit the organization.
Bar-Hayim and Berman suggest that this component of commitment corresponds with Etzioni's concept of moral involvement.

A number of studies have explored potential distinctions
between various forms of attitudinal commitment or involvement and their relationship to calculative commitment. Allen
and Mayer (1990), for example, investigated three forms of
commitment. Respectively these were, affective, continuance
and normative commitment. Affective and continuance commitment reflect the conventional attitudinal and calculative
elements of commitment respectively. Normative commitment
was defined as an employee's perceived obligation to remain
with the organization. Allen and Mayer justified these distinctions as representing the difference between wanting to remain,
(affective commitment); needing to remain, (continuance commitment), and feeling one ought to remain - (normative commitment).

Whilst acknowledging that employees may simultaneously
experience all three forms of commitment to differing levels,

Allen and Mayer argued that given the different conceptual base of each commitment construct, each may develop independently. For instance, they suggest that normative commitment may be principally a function of pre-organizational experiences such as family pressure and early organizational socialisation. In fact only continuance commitment proved to be a distinct concept. In other words, their findings did not progress beyond the basic and long recognised distinction between attitudinal and calculative commitment.

Randall, Fedor and Longenecker (1990) reached a similar conclusion. Randall et al. began by seeking to establish the meaning of commitment from the standpoint of the committed. They conducted in-depth interviews with sixteen employees selected from all levels of a medium size manufacturing plant. The principal question to respondents was 'How can you tell when someone is committed to this organization?' (p.214).

Fifteen commitment behaviours were identified such as, 'doing your work thoroughly and completely,' not being late,' and 'sharing information with others,' (p. 214). Four factors were identified as expressions of employee commitment. These were, concern for quality, willingness to make personal sacrifices for the organization, sharing information and attendance. Affective commitment predicted concern for quality, willingness to make sacrifices and information sharing whereas normative commitment predicted only sacrifice behaviours. Unlike Allen and Mayer's study, however, the continuance scale was unrelated to any outcomes. The authors concluded that affective commitment was a better predictor of behaviour than the other two forms of commitment.

Another significant aspect Randall et al.'s work is the suggestion that commitment is not necessarily expressed in the manner in which researchers operationalise the construct, (e.g., willingness to exert effort), but may reflect specific and unique organizational imperatives such as concern for quality. This might imply compliance and commitment are synonymous - a point which we return to in the discussion which concludes this book.

Commitment and Etzioni's concept of involvement

An interesting study by Johnston and Snizek (1991) starts from the proposition that organizational involvement and organizational commitment are distinct concepts, 'Strong moral involvement is but one basis of organizational commitment . . . . . individuals may be calculatively involved and organizationally committed, without exhibiting any significant moral involvement to their organization,' (p.1261). Johnston and Snizek argue that the distinction between involvement and commitment has previously been obscured by defining involvement in terms of intensity and direction. Instead, they define involvement as the nature of attachment and commitment as the strength of attachment.

Commitment was measured using Porter and Smith's (1970) scale. Involvement was measured by tapping employees' reasons for 'participating' in the organization, for example, 'Helps me meet my financial obligations,' (calculative involvement) and 'Provides me with a means of helping others,' (moral involvement), (p.1263). Task performance was measured by various quantitative indicators such as personal sales volume and number of distributors sponsored.

Calculative involvement was positively correlated with performance (r's ranging 0.27 - 0.37) whereas moral involvement was negatively related. Johnston and Snizek suggest that whilst moral involvement contributes to organization commitment, it detracts from task performance in utilitarian organizations. Otherwise the correlation between moral involvement and organizational commitment was 0.68 as against only 0.28 between calculative involvement and commitment, 'Such findings lend support to the idea that value attachment accounts for a sizeable proportion of an individual's commitment to the organization,' (p.1266).

A somewhat different approach to commitment is to differentiate between its foci and bases (Becker, 1992). The former concerns the individuals and groups to whom a person is attached. The latter concerns the motives underlying the attachment. Although both dimensions of commitment predict some variables equally well (intention to quit, satisfaction and prosocial behaviours), there are Becker argues, sufficient differences to suggest the distinction is valid. For instance, bases of commitment did not predict prosocial organizational behaviour. Moreover the two commitment constructs together account for a greater proportion of variance in important dependent variables that Porter and Smith's (1970) measure.

Discussion and conclusions

It is apparent from this review that there are major gaps in research concerning organizational commitment. Not least of these is the paucity of studies examining the impact of power. Until recently researchers have been concerned with testing and retesting the impact of a relatively narrow range of variables such as age, job satisfaction, length of service and so on. Moreover as Mathieu and Zajac (1990) note, little theoretical justification exists for the inclusion of such variables within research frameworks. Models clearly need to be broadened.

Another area which has received scant attention is the relationship between commitment and organizational characteristics. Studies reviewed here have concentrated entirely upon employing organizations and then mainly upon white collar and professional staff. Quite apart from examining commitment in coercive and normative organizations, there is also a need to compare commitment in large corporations with that in small business and high technology industries to name but a few.

The effects of organization level and occupation have also been comparatively neglected. It seems improbable that commitment levels are constant throughout the organization or that the development of involvement is the same for all types of organization members. The commitment of a migratory building operative, for example, must surely be different from that of a long serving school caretaker even though both could be classified as blue collar workers. Likewise, Gouldner (1957) has argued that professionals tend to be more committed to their profession that their organization though more recently Friedson (1984), has suggested that de-professionalisation and the development of a more egalitarian outlook is causing professionals to identify increasingly with their employers.

Are the distinctions between various forms of commitment worth making?

The emerging pattern of results raises a question about the utility of the distinction between organizational commitment and affective involvement. The various concepts, and their measures, have a tautological flavour about them. For instance in Popper and Lipshitz's (1992) study of army officers, moral values are measured by items such as 'It is important for me to work in a place where people "give their hearts" to the system,' whilst affective commitment is measured by items such as 'I like people who "give their heart" to the Israel Defence Forces,' (p. 6). It is unsurprising, therefore, that the two forms of commitment are related.

Indeed, it is doubtful whether even the distinction between the more disparate constructs of value and continuance commitment is useful. Meyer and Schoorman, 1992 observe that 'Value commitment did a very creditable job in predicting all the outcomes in the study,'(p.681). The argue that the justification for incorporating continuance commitment is that it has a stronger relationship with turnover items.

Commitment and Etzioni's theory

As far as Etzioni's theory is concerned, this review establishes that involvement is indeed potentially related to many variables besides power. This has implications for the design of the present study. The design needs to incorporate as many of the major variables affecting involvement as possible. In particular there is evidence to suggest that commitment and various measures of satisfaction including work involvement are linked. This has implications for Etzioni's theory because commitment corresponds closely with Etzioni's concept of involvement. If involvement is systematically related to organizations, and if involvement and satisfaction are related, then conceivably satisfaction might vary between organizations as well as power and involvement. This idea is explored further in the next chapter.

6 The research framework

Introduction

The purpose of this chapter is to develop the framework and hypotheses for testing Etzioni's theory. Before proceeding to do so however, it is necessary to summarise and draw together the salient theoretical and empirical issues of the preceding literature review.

Etzioni's theory outlined in Chapter One consists of the core element and related ideas. Basically the core theory may be summarised as hypothesising systematic relations between power and involvement in organizations classified as coercive, utilitarian and normative. The three forms of power thought to predominate each type of organization respectively are; coercive, remunerative and symbolic. The corresponding forms of involvement are; alienative and hostile, calculative and mildly positive and moral and extremely positive.

It was also noted in Chapter One that in addition to the core theory, Etzioni argues that power and involvement levels vary according to whether an organization is an extreme or mild example of its type. Furthermore, Etzioni suggests that there may be systematic differences in power and involvement across the whole range of organizations from extreme coercive to extreme normative types. For example, it is suggested that

97

although a hospital porter would be controlled mainly by remunerative power, the 'power mix' would contain a greater element of symbolic control than that of a factory operative because a hospital is a normative organization. Etzioni suggests that power and involvement are related to seniority even to the extent of minute differences between, say, clerks and private secretaries. A key function of this chapter is to develop these ideas into a coherent framework for testing.

The need for research

It was argued in Chapter One that a major strength of Etzioni's theory is his simplification of power concepts. Etzioni's three forms of power were identified as assets as distinct from power tactics such as use of information, persuasion manipulation and so on. The review of the literature on power in organizations contained in Chapter Four shows that research has been mainly concerned with factors determining choice of power tactics (e.g., Kipnis, Schmidit and Wilkinson, 1980). Although these studies suggest that power may not be easy to classify into schemas such as Etzioni's and, that the power in organizations may not be solely structural, they do not examine power as conceived by Etzioni. Therefore although they provide useful and interesting insights into the exercise of power in organizations, they cannot be said to be tests of Etzioni's theory.

Other studies reviewed in Chapter Four concern the impact of leader reward and punishment behaviour on satisfaction. The evidence suggests that reward behaviour is positively related to satisfaction though only Bateman and Strasser (1984) have specifically examined the impact of power on commitment. One important point highlighted by these studies and also the sociological literature (e.g., Knights and Roberts, 1982), is the existence of mental coercion in organizations. This has shown positive and negative correlations with satisfaction, and even no relationship at all (e.g., Podsakoff, 1982; Podsakoff and Todor, 1985). It is clearly an area where more research is required. Although Etzioni defines coercion as the application of physical sanctions, it was argued in Chapter One that these probably have mental ramifications. It was also suggested that mental coercion is underemphasised in Etzioni's theory and warrants investigation. Research reviewed in Chapter Four distinguishes between legitimate sanctions and illegitimate ones (known as contingency and non-contingency punishment respectively). Although results pertaining to the former may be mixed, non-contingency punishment is consistently negatively related to satisfaction. This accords with Etzioni's view of the impact of illegitimate coercion which he argues, 'Is doubly alienating, because the action is both undesirable and violates the sense of right and wrong' (Etzioni, 1968, p146). It would seem important then to incorporate both forms of sanction into the framework of this study. None of the research into power in organizations has devoted significant attention to the role of factors such as the type of organization or hierarchical level. By thus linking Etzioni's theory to the wider literature on power in organizations, the possibility of an additional contribution to knowledge is created.

It was noted in Chapter Two that Etzioni's definition and usage of the term 'involvement' identifies closely with the literature on organization commitment which is concerned with the strength of a person's attachment to the organization as evidenced by loyalty, willingness to exert effort and accept-ance of the organization's goals (Mowday Porter and Steers, 1982). With the exception of Etzioni, involvement has not been specifically linked to power in the literature though it is implied that need fulfilment is conducive to high involvement (e.g., Vroom, 1962; Maslow, 1954; Patchen, 1970). Since symbolic power concerns the satisfaction of status or ego needs, and coercion is linked to deprivation and humiliation, it is conceivable that there will be a relationship between power and involvement.

The review of research on commitment in Chapter Five concluded that there is a need to examine the impact of power on commitment in a wide range of organizations and at a variety of job levels as research has been mainly confined to white collar staff. Existing studies indicate that commitment is affected by numerous variables besides power, especially age, tenure, education and satisfaction (Mathieu and Zajac, 1990). The term satisfaction is a generic one and includes job satisfaction and work involvement. Morrow (1983) has observed that both of these are related to organizational involvement and Reichers (1985) emphasises that it is important to be mindful of the possibility of multiple involvements in organizations. Therefore although the prime focus of Etzioni's theory is on organizational involvement, it must be acknowledged that other forms of involvement are potentially significant and may also be systematically related to organizations. It is therefore important to incorporate satisfaction and the other variables listed into the theoretical framework of this research.

Approach to research

Overall, the preceding review of the literature has established that Etzioni's theory has been subject to limited empirical examination. This endorses the view presented in Chapter Three that there is a need to systematically appraise Etzioni's fundamental theoretical propositions. This is the first aim of this study.

If the role of research is to test Etzioni's theory, it is necessary to maintain close correspondence with Etzioni's concepts and hypotheses. This does not mean however that research must confine itself to Etzioni's framework. One benefit to be gained by research is the possibility of theoretical development. That is, when a theory is applied to areas not previously considered, or when it is modified in such a way that it improves its explanatory power. Logical inference or deduction may suggest the addition of new variables, or integration with other theories to achieve a more complex model (Glaser and Strauss, 1968; Etzioni, 1975; Hage, 1982). The second aim of this research therefore is to explore the possibility of theoretical development in two ways. First, by developing a more complex research model based on a logical extension of Etzioni's ideas. Second by the addition of work alienation as a new variable. Before proceeding to explain the rationale for this, it is necessary to identify and operationally define the research variables.

The research variables

Definition of research variables

It was argued in Chapter Three that a full test of Etzioni's theory requires both power and involvement to be included in the theoretical framework. Power is defined in accordance with Etzioni's (1975) own definitions as follows:

1 *Symbolic power* - the application of non material rewards such as praise and recognition.

2 *Remunerative power* - the application of material rewards including salaries and promotion.

3 *Legitimate coercion* - the application of sanctions contingent upon behaviour such as discipline or withholding promotion.

4 *Non legitimate coercion* - the arbitrary application of sanctions.

5 *Involvement* - the strength of a person's identification with an organization.

6 *Work alienation* - lack of intrinsic pride, satisfaction or meaning in work.

7 *Organization level* - a person's position within the formal organization hierarchy.

Rationale underlying definitions

The basic rationale adopted was to define variables as closely as possible to Etzioni's definitions in order to make the research a realistic test of the theory. Symbolic and remunerative power were defined in accordance with Etzioni's usage of the terms. Etzioni defines coercive power as the application of physical sanctions. It seemed this would probably be impossible to operationalise. Yet it was important to include coercion as previous research has clearly shown that it exists in organizations, though little is known about examined its impact upon involvement. Coercion was therefore defined as a psychological phenomenon. Conceivably, little would be lost by adopting this approach as it is argued that the degradations accompanying coercion, are experienced mentally as well as physically. Moreover defining coercion in this way presented the possibility of adding to Etzioni's theory.

It was noted earlier in this chapter that Etzioni suggests illegitimate coercion is more alienating than legitimate sanctions, and, that researchers have found it fruitful to distinguish between punishment that is related to performance and that which is administered arbitrarily. Accordingly both forms of coercion are included in the theoretical framework.

It was stressed in Chapter One, that the exercise of power can succeed without either intention, or capability, on the part of the power holder, so long as the power subject believes in the reality of both (Wrong,1979; Bacharach and Lawler, 1980). Power is therefore defined to include both actual and potential application. It should be noted that each of the four power types are also defined in accordance with the literature on supervisor's reward and punishment behaviour, (e.g., Sims and Syzalgyi, 1975) described in Chapter Four. This is to enable the results of this study to be related to an existing body of knowledge.

Involvement is defined after Buchanan (1974) and Porter et al. (1974) in accordance with the literature on organizational commitment outlined in Chapters Two and Five of this book. Defining involvement in this way not only differentiates clearly between work and organizational involvement, it also makes it possible to contribute to the literature on organizational commitment.

Work alienation is defined after Miller (1968) and Seeman (1971). It is intended to reflect what Kanungo (1982) calls the contemporary view of sociologists who regard it as a form of disappointment with work which fails to provide intrinsic need satisfaction, or opportunities for self direction, and self expression. This is consistent with Etzioni's view of alienation as resulting from frustration of worker's needs and expectations on the job and their lack of power and control (Etzioni, 1968c). It is acknowledged that this definition overlaps with the concept of job satisfaction; what is important here is to differentiate between orientations to work and orientations to the organization. The rationale for the inclusion of work alienation as a new correlate is explained further on in this Chapter

Organization level is included as a potential second dimension of Etzioni's theory. The reasons for this are explained later in this Chapter. Here it is sufficient to note that the term relates to hierarchical aspects of organizations.

Research aim one: a model for testing the core theory

Alternative approaches to testing the core theory

The first aim of this research is to test the fundamental propositions of Etzioni's theory. One option would have been apply the basic model and test whether each type of organization relied on the form of power specified by Etzioni, and whether involvement related concomitantly. Whilst this might have made a useful contribution to knowledge, potentially more could be learnt by logical pursuit of Etzioni's predictions towards the development of a more comprehensive, yet still simple, model based on the idea of systematic relations between power and involvement across the whole range of organizations. This would not only facilitate testing of the basic theory, but could itself be developed to enable a much wider exploration of Etzioni's ideas.

Towards an extended model of power and involvement

Although Etzioni has tended to regard his three categories of organization as exclusive in that each is identified with a particular form of power and involvement, the logic of his hypotheses suggests these variables relate systematically between all three types of organization.

The argument is as follows. Take for example symbolic power. If it is highest in normative organizations then it is probably lowest in coercive ones. This is on the basis of the argument that coercion renders an appeal to values useless, and therefore symbolic power is wasted upon those already alienated. However, it was argued in Chapter Two that, although utilitarian organizations may rely heavily upon their power to remunerate, it is in their interests to make some use of symbolic power as it is a cost effective means of generating involvement. In other words, it is logical to conceive symbolic power as incrementally related across the range of archetypal normative, utilitarian and coercive organizations.

The same reasoning can be applied to coercion which, it is suggested, will relate to organizations in the opposite way to symbolic power. According to Etzioni, coercive organizations rely upon it as their main means of control. This suggests coercion will be at least higher in coercive organizations than either utilitarian or normative types. If as Etzioni says, coercion destroys involvement, then normative organizations are the least likely of the three to use it as they need high involvement.

Utilitarian organizations do not require such high involvement, nor are they able to coerce employees to the level permissable in, say, a prison. However, they are able to sanction employees to some extent by applying remunerative powers coercively. This suggests they would fall somewhere between on a scale of low to high reliance on coercion.

This idea is not applicable to remunerative power in quite the same way as neither coercive, nor many normative organizations, possess the requisite resources. However it seems reasonable to suggest that if reliance on coercion increases towards the normative end of the range, reliance on remuneration declines because there is less need for it. Likewise it is suggested that its use declines towards the coercive end of the range of organizations as reliance is placed on force. It is acknowledged that prison inmates often perform work in return for pay, however Etzioni clearly argues that coercion is the predominant means of control.

Given Etzioni's theory of a link between power and involvement, it seems reasonable to suggest that involvement also varies systematically across the range of organizations. The reasoning for this is based on the assumption that involvement is positively associated with symbolic power, and negatively related to coercion. If reliance on symbolic power increases towards the normative end of the range and coercion decreases, (or vice versa), then it follows that involvement will vary from

105

high to low between normative, utilitarian and coercive organizations respectively. The first research aim, therefore, is to test whether power and involvement relate systematically across all three types of organization.

Research aim two: applying Etzioni's theory to intermediate organizations

The model developed so far assumes the existence of organizations that are archetypal examples of their respective classifications. It was noted in Chapter One, however, that Etzioni has suggested that systematic differences in power and involvement exist between organizations within each of the three types. For example, Etzioni argued that inmates in milder coercive organizations like open prisons would be less alienated than those incarcerated in concentration camps and exposed to extreme coercion.

If coercion, symbolic power and involvement relate to one another as suggested, then it is possible that the theory of power and involvement can also be applied to intermediate organizations. The more an organization leans towards the normative end of the range, the greater the reliance on symbolic power, whilst reliance on coercion decreases and involvement increases. Conversely the more an organization leans towards the utilitarian part of the range, the less it relies on symbolic power and the more it relies on coercion. Remunerative power is different and more likely to relate in a curvilinear fashion. That is, highest in extreme utilitarian organizations and decreasing towards both the coercive and normative end of the range. Involvement varies concomitantly. This would mean for example that lower participants in an extreme religious sect would be more involved than their counterparts in borderline normative/utilitarian organization such as a firm of architects.

Whilst it is acknowledged that the review of research in coercive organizations indicated this idea may be an oversimplification, (e.g., Bettelheim, 1943; Hepburn, 1985), it has an intuitive appeal and, has been subject to only limited empirical investigation. It therefore seems important to explore it further with a wider range of organizations, operationalising power as well as involvement.

Accordingly, the second aim of the research is to test the relevance of Etzioni's theory to 'intermediate' organizations.

Research aim three: exploring power and involvement within organizations

Etzioni's theory is based upon the lower participants of organizations. It was noted in Chapter One, however, that Etzioni suggests senior managers tend to be more symbolically controlled and less coerced than employees in the lower echelons. Etzioni even suggests that involvement varies between groups of staff who are only slightly apart on the organizational hierarchy. Private secretaries suggests Etzioni, will be a degree more symbolically controlled than ordinary clerks. There is some empirical support for this. Beyer and Trice (1984) found that senior managers were more likely to escape punishment whilst Clegg and Wall (1981) reported that commitment was positively related to seniority.

It is argued, therefore, that this implies the possibility of systematic relations between power and involvement within organizations. It is thus necessary to develop these primary indications into a systematic framework for testing. If senior managers are afforded greater symbolic control and freedom from punishment than those at the lower echelons, assuming power and involvement are related, it follows that they will also be more involved. If minute differences in the level of symbolic control exist between clerks and private secretaries, then why not between all ranks? In turn variations in symbolic control also connote variations in coercion, remunerative power and involvement. The indications are thus of an incremental relationship between power and involvement within organizations. Reliance upon symbolic power increases with seniority whilst remunerative and coercive power decreases. Correspondingly, involvement rises with seniority. Hence the third research aim is to examine Etzioni's theory within organizations.

Research aim four: work alienation as a new variable

The final aim of the research is to explore the possibility of adding a new variable to Etzioni's theory. The reasoning for this is derived from the literature. In Chapter Three it was noted that work alienation was lower amongst scientists working in a university like atmosphere, than those engaged in a more utilitarian research and development department (Miller, 1967). Etzioni (1975) attributes this to a greater degree of symbolic control in the case of the former. Although it is argued that this was never empirically established, it nevertheless suggests the possibility of a link between power and work alienation.

Studies on supervisors' use of rewards and punishments reviewed in Chapter Four indicate a relationship between reward and various measures of satisfaction including satisfaction with supervision and co-workers. Whilst accepting that it could be said that the relationship between satisfaction and work alienation is tenuous, equally it could be argued that someone who is alienated from work is less likely to be satisfied with their supervisor and co workers than someone who is more involved. This too is suggestive of a link between power and work alienation.

The literature on organizational commitment shows that there is a relationship between commitment and job satisfaction (e.g.,

Bateman and Strasser, 1984; Curry et al. 1986). Low job satisfaction is sufficiently close to the concept of work alienation to lend credence to the idea of a link between involvement and work alienation. More direct evidence is presented by Morrow (1983) who observed that organizational involvement and constructs of work involvement are related.

There are, therefore, indications in the literature to suggest the possibility of a relationship between power and work alienation and related constructs, and between organizational involvement and forms of work involvement. Assuming that power relates systematically to organizations over a range of compliance structures, and assuming involvement does the same, then it follows that if work alienation is related to both power and involvement, it too will vary systematically by organization type.

It was noted in Chapter Two that Kanungo (1979) has argued work involvement and work alienation are opposite sides of the coin. Morrow (1983) has observed that all the well known constructs of work involvement overlap. Basically the evidence is that rewards and organizational involvement are positively related to constructs of work involvement. Conversely, low work alienation has been linked to high symbolic power.

This would mean that across a range of organizations from coercive to normative, work alienation would be highest at the extreme coercive end of the range and decrease towards the normative end. Similarly within organizations, work alienation would be highest amongst the lower echelons and decrease with seniority.

Predicted relationships between the research variables

Relations between power, involvement, work alienation and organization type

The predicted relations between power, involvement, work alienation, organization type and job level may be summarised as follows:

1   *Symbolic power* - is expected to be lowest in the coercive organization and increase towards the normative end of the power scale. It is expected to be positively associated with seniority within organizations.

2   *Remunerative power* - is expected to be highest in the utilitarian organization, decreasing towards the coercive and normative end of the power scale. It is expected to be negatively associated with seniority within organizations.

3   *Coercion* - is expected to be highest in the coercive organization, decreasing towards the normative end of the power scale. It is expected to be negatively associated with seniority within organizations.

4   *Involvement* - is expected to be lowest in the coercive organization, increasing towards the normative end of the power scale. It is expected to be positively associated with seniority within organizations.

5 *Work alienation* - is expected to be highest in the coercive organization, decreasing towards the normative end of the power scale. It is expected to be negatively related with seniority within organizations.

The predictions pertaining to variations of power, involvement and work alienation between organizations are summarised in Figure 3. Those pertaining to variations within organizations are summarised in Figure 4.

	ORGANIZATION		
	COERCIVE	UTILITARIAN	NORMATIVE
SYMBOLIC POWER	Low	Medium	High
REMUNERATIVE POWER	Low	High	Low
COERCION	High	Medium	Low
INVOLVEMENT	Low	Medium	High
WORK ALIENATION	High	Medium	Low

**Figure 3   Predicted relations of research variables
between organizations**

	ORGANIZATION LEVEL		
	LOWER PARTICIPANTS	MIDDLE MANAGEMENT	SENIOR MANAGEMENT
SYMBOLIC POWER	Low	Medium	High
REMUNERATIVE POWER	High	Medium	Low
COERCION	High	Medium	Low
INVOLVEMENT	Low	Medium	High
WORK ALIENATION	High	Medium	Low

Figure 4   Predicted relations of research variables within organizations

Interrelations between power, involvement and work alienation

In view of Etzioni's theory of power and involvement, plus evidence in the literature of positive relations between rewards and involvement and various form of employee satisfaction, it is anticipated that symbolic and remunerative power will correlate positively with involvement and negatively with work alienation. Conversely both contingency and non-contingency coercion are expected to relate negatively to involvement and positively to work alienation. Stronger correlations for non-contingency coercion are expected in view of its arbitrary nature.

Control variables

The literature on involvement suggests that it is influenced by many variables besides power. Amongst the most important are age, sex, education and tenure (Mathieu and Zajac, 1990). These were included in the study to act as controls. Closeness of supervision and amount of choice in work were also included as being of potential significance in view of their links with satisfaction and need fulfilment.

Research hypotheses

From the foregoing predictions the following research hypotheses were derived:

1   Power varies systematically by organization type.

2   Involvement varies systematically by organization type.

3   Work alienation varies systematically by organization type.

4   Power varies systematically by organization level.

5   Involvement varies systematically by organization level.

6   Work alienation varies systematically by organization level.

7   Power and involvement are related.

Specific hypotheses are stated in Chapter Nine.

Summary

This Chapter has identified the key variables and aims of the study and explained the rationale underlying the construction of the research model. This involves a logical extension of Etzioni's propositions supported by evidence contained within the literature. The result is a development of Etzioni's theory represented as consisting of a threefold, discrete set of congruent compliance structures towards a model proposing relations between power and involvement across the whole range of organizations plus the addition of work alienation as a potential new variable. It is argued that this retains all the simplicity of Etzioni's original whilst enabling more complex and far reaching hypotheses to be tested. Four research aims were specified: to test Etzioni's basic theory; to apply the theory to intermediate organizations; to apply the theory to compliance structures within organizations; and to test the potential of work alienation as a new variable. In the next Chapter the research design and research organizations are described.

7 The research organizations

Introduction

It was said in the last chapter that the aim of this research is to examine the relationship between power, involvement and work alienation across a range of organizations and also between staff at different hierarchical levels within organizations. This required an analysis of the relationships between variables in order to identify concomitant variation. Consequently, a key factor which dictated the choice of design and methodology was the need to make systematic comparisons between organizations and sub-groups within them.

The method adopted in this research was therefore a cross sectional questionnaire survey. All of the major approaches to organizational research were considered. The advantage of experimentation is that it is the technique likely to establish causal relations among variables. The disadvantage is that the range of an experiment is comparatively narrow. Interviews can facilitate and in-depth exploration of the study phenomena and may yield rich insights. However it would have been at the expense of more objective systematic comparisons as interview data tend to lend themselves less readily to numerical analyses.

Selecting the research organizations

The research aims and hypotheses required comparisons between Etzioni's archetypal organizations and also the inclusion of one or more intermediate organizations within the model. One or more of the research organizations also needed to be large enough to facilitate the exploration of compliance structures between lower and higher echelons.

Five organizations participated in the survey. A voluntary group represented an extreme normative type; a factory stood surrogate as a utilitarian archetype and a sample of ex-prison inmates represented a coercive setting. A college stood for an intermediate normative organization and a City Works Department represented an intermediate utilitarian type.

The rationale for choice was as follows. Comparison of Etzioni's three archetypes required the inclusion of a coercive organization, a typically utilitarian organization and a typically normative one. Etzioni (1968a) lists coercive organizations as including concentration camps, jails and coercive unions. Of these, state prisons are a good example of a coercive organization. Etzioni lists factories as examples of extreme utilitarian organizations, hence the choice. According to Etzioni, normative organizations range from professional business organizations which he regards as comparatively mild examples, to extreme religious and political sects. Voluntary organizations veer towards the extreme end of the spectrum. It seemed that choice of extreme examples would enable a realistic assessment of Etzioni's basic theory, the first and foremost aim of the research.

Public bureaucracies are regarded by Etzioni (1968a) as borderline utilitarian/normative types whilst colleges and universities are seen as about half way along the normative spectrum. Hence not only were the intermediate organizations sufficiently apart from the archetypes to enable variations to be detected, but they was also a significant degree of difference between the two intermediate types. This meant that a range of four distinct organizations on the utilitarian/normative spectrum could be explored.

Another reason for the inclusion of three large employing organizations in the survey (college, City Works and factory), was to facilitate exploration of compliance structures within organizations. The coercive and archetypal normative organizations were excluded partly because Etzioni's predictions are directed towards senior managers of employing organizations, and partly because the structure of these organizations is too flat to obtain realistic samples from middle and senior echelons.

Description of the participant organizations

Normative archetype: the voluntary group (W.R.V.S.)

The Women's Royal Voluntary Service (W.R.V.S.) was established in anticipation of the Second World War to alleviate human suffering and distress. During the war, the W.R.V.S. organized mobile canteens, distributed clothes to people who had lost their possessions and cared for the bereaved and distressed. The organization became known as 'The army which Hitler forgot' (Beauman; 1977, Greaves, 1948).

The peacetime role of the W.R.V.S. still primarily revolves round responding to emergency and disaster. Members' prime role consists of supporting other emergency services by providing food and rest and comforting victims and their relatives. The organization also supports the elderly in the community through its 'Meals on Wheels' service and assists at charity events.

The W.R.V.S. is funded by the Home Office but all members are volunteers. Every branch has a leader and other officials but all members are regarded as equal. The only rewards are a Long Service Certificate, and a Long Service Medal awarded for a combination of length of service and number of hours worked.

117

Contrary to what the organization's title suggests, membership is open to both sexes. The branch which participated in the survey had a substantial proportion of males in the membership.

Intermediate normative organization: the college

The college employs approximately 900 full time, academic and non-academic staff. It is controlled by a Governing Body composed of local councillors, and nominees from local industry, service and voluntary organizations, though the Principal has responsibility for overall co-ordination, control, and day to day management. Funding comes from central and local government and increasingly from courses organised on an economic cost basis.

The staff are divided into academic and non-academic. Academic staff include the Principal, Vice-Principals, Heads of Department and Lecturers. Non-academic staff consist of administrators, clerical, technical, secretarial and blue collar groups. Senior academic staff tend to be promoted from lecturer grades. Transfer between academics and non-academics or white collar and blue collar staff is rare.

Courses offered by the college range from basic literacy to degree level. The main pressure on the organization is financial, both to maintain and in some cases increase staff student ratios and to boost income. However the college is located in an area of high unemployment and urban deprivation where education is of high priority. Therefore, within these constraints, it operates without any immediate or likely threat of closure or drastic financial cuts. A 'no compulsory redundancy' agreement operates for all staff. When interviewed, the Vice Principal remarked that dismissal was not really seen as an option, especially for academic staff.

City Works employs approximately 180 white collar staff and 1200 blue collar labourers and craftsmen. It is responsible for refuse disposal, upkeep of council property, highways and drainage and vehicle maintenance. The staff are composed of engineers, stores officers, wages and bonus costing clerks, inspectors, technicians, quantity surveyors, refuse officers, clock menders, labourers and craftsmen plus administrative and clerical support staff. A bonus system operates for most of the labourers and craftsmen. The director is an engineer but there is no organizational tradition or statutory requirement that would prevent a non-professional from being appointed to this role. Similarly, it would be possible for a craftsman to attain a senior management position without obtaining further educational qualifications.

City Works was described as being under intense and continuous pressure to meet unit costs in order to compete with the private sector and meet legal requirements of a five percent return on capital. The commitment required from all staff was summarised by the personnel manager as 'perform or out'. In one instance thirty days sickness absence resulted in dismissal. Although the trade unions protested, they were overruled by their own members who were not prepared to tolerate nonproductive colleagues.

Notwithstanding these pressures, City Works is a local government organization and regarded by the City Council as a service department. This is reflected in the relatively advantageous conditions of service compared with those in the private sector. The Council maintains a policy of being a good employer. A 'No compulsory redundancy' agreement is in force; wage rates, sickness benefits and superannuation schemes are negotiated nationally and clearly specified. These include benefits such as paternity leave, a generous training provision and a commitment to a policy of equal opportunities. Almost all staff are members of a Trades Union; industrial relations are based on co-operation and joint problem solving.

Archetypal utilitarian organization: the factory

The factory is part of a national group manufacturing confectionery. It employs over 1000 staff, in an area of high unemployment. The majority of these are process workers. Staff at intermediate levels consist mainly of chargehands and supervisors. Senior management include sales, personnel, finance, and production managers. The factory manager began his career as an apprentice and many other senior staff were promoted from clerical positions though the younger ones tend to be professionally qualified graduates. None of the senior staff is in a union.

The recession and development of new technology, have resulted in successive staff reductions through compulsory redundancy. The company regards itself as a good employer inasmuch as it operates an equal opportunities policy and abides by the Advisory Conciliation and Arbitration Service (A.C.A.S.) Codes of Practice on redundancy and dismissal. However, the personnel manager emphasised that staff were not regarded as members of the organization, but as employees. Informal conversations with shop floor operatives also suggested a somewhat instrumental approach beneath the formal policy statements. For example, they said morning shift starts at 7.30 a.m. Those arriving later than 8 a.m. are locked out. It was also clear that there was considerable distrust between the trade unions and management, so much so that it was feared that this study might be interpreted as a ploy of management to obtain information about its work force for unscrupulous purposes.

Coercive organization: N.A.C.R.O.

An organization known as N.A.C.R.O. (National Association for the Care and Resettlement of Offenders) was approached for access to ex offenders. N.A.C.R.O acted as intermediaries by putting the researcher in touch with people recently released from custody. They were in a good position to do so as N.A.C.R.O. exists as a point of contact for everyone released from prison. N.A.C.R.O.'s activities include running literacy classes, sponsoring employment schemes and the maintenance of close links with the probation services.

Defining organization levels

One of the research aims was to explore the possibility of systematic relations between power, involvement and work alienation within organizations using the three employing organizations involved in the survey. The definition of organization levels was guided by the theoretical models of Parsons (1960) and Mintzberg (1979). Parsons views organizations as consisting of three levels or sub organizations; technical, managerial and institutional. The technical level performs the organization's basic function, teaching a class, assembling a product, typing letters and so on. The managerial level decides what will be taught, how classrooms will be allocated etc. The managerial level is controlled by the institutional structure. This may take many forms including for example, elected members and boards of directors. Essentially it is the mediator between the managerial and technical structures and the community.

Mintzberg's model also consists of three levels: operating core, middle level and strategic apex. The operating core corresponds to Parson's technical level. The middle level links the strategic apex to the operating core. This ranges from senior managers to first line supervisors. Its role is to collect feedback and intervene in decisions. Two further middle level categories suggested by Mintzberg are the technostructure which imposes standardization, and the support staff who enable the operating core to function. The strategic apex is concerned with the formulation of policy and coordination of the total organization. Mintzberg views this role as being discharged by full time paid executives of the organization unlike Parson's who ascribes these functions to what are often a part-time, elected directorate.

Applying theory to the research design

Etzioni has not developed a typology of organizational hierarchies, he simply suggests that there will be differences in power and involvement between the various echelons. The value of Parson's and Mintzberg's models is that they facilitate a systematic approach to testing Etzioni's ideas.

 Accordingly the design was based upon a threefold classification. Lower participants were defined to include staff at the technical level or operating core. Middle management were defined in accordance with Mintzberg's middle level. Technostructure and support staff were subsumed under this category as it was felt that it would overly complicate the research to differentiate between different kinds of middle level staff. Mintzberg's idea of the strategic apex seemed more consonant with Etzioni's concept of senior management than Parson's institutional level and so it was used to define higher participants.

Sampling strategy

The sampling strategy adopted aimed to reduce as far as practicable the possibility of sampling bias and error by the use of samples as large as possible (including a census), and stratification using a combination of probability and non-probability techniques. A further consideration in sampling was the requirements of parametric statistical techniques which require sub sets of atleast thirty (Roscoe, 1975).

Sampling the research organizations

Data obtained through N.A.C.R.O. were a natural sample. A questionnaire was offered to everyone in contact with the organization who had served a custodial sentence within the last year. The aim was to obtain atleast thirty returns. A census approach was used with the W.R.V.S. A questionnaire was posted to the thirty-eight members on the emergency duty rota who constituted the hard core membership of the organization.

The college, City Works and the factory were more complicated to sample as it was necessary to ensure adequate representation of lower, middle and senior levels. This was achieved by attempting to obtain as large a sample as possible of each sub group (minimum of thirty wherever possible), and, by employing stratified sampling.

Strengths and weaknesses of the research design

The advantage of the design was that it enabled testing not only of Etzioni's basic theory but also the validity of a more complex model. The voluntary organization, the factory and the prison sample were all good examples of their respective archetypes which meant that testing of the basic theory was soundly based. The disadvantage of the voluntary organization and prison sample was that they were unsuitable for an examination of compliance structures within organizations. The alternative would have been to seek access to the church, a somewhat less extreme examples of a normative organization. Given that this aspect of the research could still be explored in three of the organizations, it seemed better to obtain data from good exam-

123

ples of coercive and normative organizations albeit at the sacrifice of some elegance.

The same argument applies to the prison sample. Whilst it might have been possible to obtain data from three levels from a quasi coercive organization such as the military, to do so would have been to compromise on a critical aspect of the research. It seemed better to reserve adjustments to secondary aims of the study.

It was recognised that sample sizes from both organizations would be small. However, all the indications from the voluntary organization suggested that it would be feasible to achieve atleast thirty returns. Not only would this be sufficient for statistical analysis, but thirty would actually be representative of almost eighty percent of the group. In the case of the prison sample, the total prison population is only around 40, 000 and therefore a return of thirty represents a reasonable proportion.

It could be argued that data from ex-inmates is less reliable than from those actually in prison. The counter argument is that it might actually be more reliable as respondents were no longer under the power of prison authorities. It was clear from the researcher's informal discussions with respondents that their memories of incarceration were vivid.

Another issue was the selection of a college as an example of an intermediate normative organization. In recent years economic pressures have forced colleges to become more financially conscious and academic staff have from time to time resorted to industrial action in support of pay claims. Arguably this means that colleges can no longer be regarded as normative organizations. The same however could be argued for hospitals which are also classified by Etzioni as normative organizations. Besides, the issue was not so much whether colleges can be regarded as normative organizations, but whether they relied more on symbolic control and less on coercion than an organization more orientated to production than service provision.

The adoption of a three fold system of classifying organizations had the virtue of simplicity whilst facilitating a thorough examination of the theory. The major difficulty here lay in specifying which staff should be classed as lower participants and which should be assigned to the middle ranks. For example should college lecturers be treated as lower participants? If so, should college clerical, secretarial and blue collar staff be included in the sample? Amongst the latter should white collar staff be included, or should only the blue collar staff be regarded as lower participants?

The dilemma was resolved on the basis that it seemed more useful to compare like groups with like. Whereas it might not come as a surprise to discover that college lecturers were more symbolically controlled than factory operatives, it would be interesting to see whether blue collar workers in a college were more symbolically controlled than their counterparts in a factory. This approach also had the advantage of being consistent with the spectral model of organizations. (In fact although the design was based on comparison of homogeneous groups, the actual analysis was more wide ranging and included a substitution of college lecturers as lower participants.)

It was impossible to achieve this level of homogeneity amongst middle management. The only way in which it would have been possible would have been to select organizations so similar as to defeat the purpose of the research. One problem in applying Mintzberg's category of middle management is that it embraces a wide range of staff from first line supervisors to senior managers just below the strategic apex.

Although the category may be wide, nonetheless it could be argued that there are fundamental differences between non supervisory and supervisory personnel however low the position of the latter on the hierarchy and that the distinction is significant if crude. One option was to create a fourth category by dividing middle management into two groups but this was rejected because it would make the design too complicated.

Research which relies upon the return of questionnaires has to allow for the possibility of a low response. For this reason as many of the target population as possible within each organization and stratum were sampled as it was felt that the potential sacrifice of efficiency, was far outweighed by the danger of obtaining an inadequate sample size. Survey administration varied from organization to organization. Basically questionnaires were administered by post or in person either by the researcher or the personnel manager of the organization. All questionnaires were accompanied by an explanatory letter and a pre-addressed confidential return envelope.

Summary

The research design was dictated by the research problem which required comparisons between archetypal and intermediate organizations plus exploration of compliance structures between lower and higher echelons.

Archetypal coercive, utilitarian and normative organizations were represented by a sample of ex inmates, a factory and voluntary organization respectively. A college and a City Works organization served as examples of intermediate organizations. Data from middle and senior ranks were collected from the three employing organizations.

The sampling strategy sought to eliminate sample bias and reduce sample error. To achieve this, where possible a census was taken of sub groups or stratified sampling was employed using a combination of probability and non probability techniques.

It was argued that the key strengths of the design are that it facilitates a relevant, thorough and systematic examination of the core theory as well as enabling wider exploration.

8 Measuring the research variables

Introduction

Lawler (1985) points out that in Organizational Behaviour it is all too easy for results to be more the product of the methodology than the phenomena under study. This criticism was levelled against many of the sociological studies reviewed in Chapter Three. It was argued that these were partial as few had measured power and those that had suffered from weaknesses of poor construct definition, or failure to explore the 'power subject's' perceptions. Similarly many studies based on involvement utilized esoteric measures, many of them unvalidated. Consequently their conclusions are questionable. Similar reservations apply to studies examining power from the standpoint of the powerholder instead of the power target and to measures which tap what a power holder 'can' do as distinct from what the power target believes the power holder 'will' do. Since the research was based on the concept of concomitant variation, precision required the use of identical measures for all organizations.

Consequently major criteria in selecting measures were:

1   Evidence of acceptable psychometric properties.

2   Close correspondence with Etzioni's concepts.

3   Measurement of attitudes and beliefs from the stand point of the power target.

4   Applicability across a range of organizations.

The implications of these criteria are discussed later, what can be said at the outset is that they precluded consideration of some of the more abstract or context specific methods of measurement noted in the literature survey.

Measurement of power

Measuring power was one of the most difficult aspects of the research as so little work had been done in this field. The literature revealed no measurement scales directly related to Etzioni's three forms of power. Available measures tended to be designed for use in specific settings such as a prison, and were not adaptable for any other type of organization, or were too far removed from Etzioni's concepts.

One option would have been to exclude power and base the research on involvement alone; this was an approach used by many of the sociological studies reviewed in Chapter Three. Although the discovery, or non discovery, of systematic variations in involvement between coercive, utilitarian, normative and intermediate organizations would have provided a partial test of the theory, it would have meant leaving the question of a link between power and involvement unanswered. Consequently it was deemed important to find some way of measuring power.

The measure used was Sim's and Syzilagyi's (1975) 'Supervisor Reward and Punishment Behavior Scale'. (See Drummond (1989) for details of pilot studies utilising other measures.) As its title suggests, Sim's and Szilagyi's scale measures reward power and coercion. The scale's psychometric properties were promising with reported reliability coefficients ranging from 0.70 to 0.93, and freedom from social desirability bias (Sims and Szilagyi, 1975).

An item by item examination of the construct validity against Etzioni's definitions of symbolic and remunerative power revealed some potentially accurate operationalisations of the constructs. For example, 'Your supervisor would give you special recognition if your work performance was especially good.' This seemed to encapsulate recognition which is regarded by Etzioni as an example of symbolic power. Likewise the item 'Your supervisor would recommend that you be promoted if your work was better than others who were otherwise equally qualified,' seemed consonant with Etzioni's concept of remunerative power. Items which appeared unrelated to Etzioni's concepts were eliminated. For example, 'Your supervisor would lend a sympathetic ear if you had a complaint.' Moreover a pilot study identified some ambiguities in that some of the items intended to measure reward behaviours could be interpreted as coercive. For instance, one respondent reading the item, 'Your supervisor would help you get a transfer if you asked for one,' thinking of her own supervisor said: 'Definitely true; old devil, he'd see you got a transfer alright.' Such items were also eliminated.

The scale used in the present study is contained in Appendix One. Four items were selected to represent symbolic power, namely:

1.   Paying a compliment.

2.   Favourable report to superior.

3.   Increased responsibilities.

4.   The items representing remunerative power were:

a. Patronage.

b. Promotion.

c. Training.

d. Fair evaluation of performance.

Since the items representing symbolic power are potentially a precursor of promotion or pay increase in employing organizations, arguably these are ultimately based on remunerative control. The difficulty with this view is that it obscures the subtleties of power and the interrelations and interactions between different types of power. Praise, recognition and so forth are gestures indicating trust and confidence and therefore their significance is symbolic. Ultimately what it might show is that in employing organizations rely to some extent upon symbolic rewards as these require fewer resources. After all, it is seldom possible to increase someone's salary each time they do a good job. Likewise, supervisors may have little control over promotion. A prime advantage of Sim's and Szilagyi's scale is its ability to accommodate supervisor's varying responses to employees, and allow for the possibility of multiple applications of power unlike ranking methods often used in conjunction with French and Raven's typology (Podsakoff and Schriescheim, 1985).

All six items relating to contingency punishment were used to measure coercion, that is:

1. Informal reprimand for lateness.

2. Dismissal for unauthorised absence.

3. Informal reprimand for poor work.

4. Withhold pay increase.

5. Formal reprimand for poor work.

6. Block promotion.

Four items representing non-contingency punishment behaviour developed by Podsakoff (cited in Podsakoff, Todor and Grover, 1984) were added to represent illegitimate coercion. This scale had reported reliability coefficients ranging 0.80 to 0.93 (Podsakoff, Todor and Skov, 1982). It concerns perceived propensity of a supervisor to punish unjustly, for example, 'Your supervisor is often critical of your work even when you perform well.'

Measurement of organizational involvement

It was argued in Chapter Three that Etzioni's treatment of involvement is consonant with the concept of organizational commitment which focuses upon an individual's feelings towards the organization. The critical issue therefore was to choose a scale with a distinct organizational focus as it was intended to measure orientations to work (work alienation) separately. Whereas with power there was a dearth of measures, with involvement the opposite was true, there being numerous involvement and involvement-related scales to choose from. The need for a scale with an organizational focus, however, narrowed the choice by eliminating consideration of involvement related measures such as Central Life Interest and Protestant Ethic in favour of alternatives which were much more specifically related to Etzioni's concept of organizational involvement.

Involvement as a single or multi-dimensional concept

It was necessary to decide whether to treat involvement as a single or a multi-dimensional concept and measure moral, calculative and alienative involvement separately. In his review of compliance studies Etzioni (1975) has implied that for practical purposes, a uni-dimensional approach is valid. Further, it is unclear from recent studies whether a multi-dimensional approach really is useful. Mayer and Allen (1992), for instance, note that value commitment is a good predictor. Value commitment is closely related to the general concept of organization commitment (Johnston and Snizek, 1991). The main justification for measuring continuance commitment separately is its ability to predict turnover. Turnover was tangential to the present study. More importantly, scales purporting to measure continuance commitment may actually represent moral involvement. For example, the scale of calculative involvement developed by Hrebiniak and Alluto (1972) taps an employee's propensity to leave the organization for inducements including more pay and friendlier co-workers. Arguably these items really measure loyalty which is actually a facet of moral involvement (Penley and Gould, 1988).

The most popular measure of organizational commitment is Porter and Smith's (1970) 'Organizational Commitment Questionnaire.' Despite impressive evidence of the scale's psychometric properties, it was unacceptable to respondents (Drummond, 1992,a). Commitment was therefore measured using Cook and Wall's (1980) nine item scale which was designed for a catholic audience. The scale taps the same constructs as Porter and Smith's measure, that is, loyalty, willingness to exert effort on behalf of the organization and identification with the organization. There is satisfactory evidence of its psychometric properties (Cook and Wall, 1980; Clegg and Wall, 1981).

Measurement of work alienation

It was noted in Chapter Two that work alienation and low work involvement may be viewed as synonymous. This implied a choice of either as a measure. The difficulty with measurement is that the overlapping nature of the construct is sometimes reflected in the measures (Morrow and Melroy, 1986). For example, Lodahl and Kejner's (1965) scale suffers from items loading onto two factors, personal value orientation and specific job motivation (Cook et al., 1981). A further constraint was relevance. For instance, Cook and Wall's (1980) work involvement scale asks respondents whether they would continue to work if they won a large sum of money and how they would feel about being unemployed. Such questions were inappropriate for either a coercive or a voluntary organization.

Miller's (1967) work alienation scale was used as it measures intrinsic pride and meaning in work. There was satisfactory evidence of internal reliability with Spearman Brown coefficients averaging 0.80 (Cook et al., 1981) and evidence of discriminant validity with correlations of -0.72 and -0.43 with job satisfaction and Index B of Patchen's Job Involvement respectively (Rousseau, 1977). A further advantage was that the scale had been used in the study of alienation amongst work scientists cited in Chapter Three.

Adaptation of measures

The questionnaire for the voluntary organization required only amendments to the nomenclature. These were devised in consultation with the W.R.V.S. Branch Organizer. It was necessary to amend the wording of some of the power scale items to make them appropriate for ex-inmates. Amendments were made in consultation with the N.A.C.R.O. manager himself an ex-inmate. On the power items, for example, the statement 'You would receive a reprimand from your supervisor if you were late in coming to work,' was re-worded to 'You would receive a reprimand from the warders if you broke the rules.' (The amended scale is shown in Appendix 2.)

The work alienation and organizational commitment scales required only amendments to the nomenclature. Two items of the latter, (willingness to leave for a more money or better job security), were irrelevant to both ex-inmates and W.R.V.S. members and consequently were eliminated.

Pearson correlation coefficients were computed to check the level of correspondence between seven and nine item versions of the organizational commitment scale in the three research organizations where these were relevant, that is, college, factory and City Works respectively. These ranged between 0.94 and 0.99 ($p<0.001$) suggesting that deletion of two items would make very little difference to the results.

Choice of work was measured by one item, 'In general how much choice do you have concerning the work you do?' The response categories ranged from 'Almost no choice;' 'Some,' to 'Almost complete choice. Closeness of supervision was measured by one item asking respondents to indicate how often they saw their supervisor. The response categories ranged from 'Works with me all the time;' 'Several times a week,' to 'Less than once a week.'

Summary

This chapter has described how power, involvement and work alienation were measured. The main criteria in selecting measures was their relevance to Etzioni's concepts, their psychometric properties and applicability to all of the research organizations. It was considered important to pursue research from the standpoint of the power target.

Power was measured using items from Sims and Syzilagyi's

(1975) 'Supervisor Reward and Punishment Behavior Scale'. Non-contingency punishment behaviour was measured using items from a scale developed by Podsakoff (Podsakoff, Todor and Grover, 1984). Involvement was measured using items from Cook and Wall's (1980) 'Organizational Commitment Questionnaire.' Work alienation was measured using Miller's (1967) scale. In the next chapter the results of the research are presented.

9 Analysis and results

Introduction

This chapter contains the results of the research. The following analyses concentrate upon the lower participants as it is with these that Etzioni's theory is primarily concerned. Where appropriate, however, analysis focuses upon each organization as a whole as well as exploring levels of power and involvement amongst various sub groups.

Data were analyzed mainly by Oneway Analysis of Variance (A.N.O.V.A) and Tukey's *a posteriori* test. Details of the preliminary data analyses including tests means and standard deviations of the main study variables are contained in Appendix 4 and reliability estimates, (r's ranging from 0.63 - 0.88), in Appendix 5.

Testing hypotheses linking power involvement and work alienation by organization

Sub hypotheses

1   Symbolic power will be highest in the voluntary organization, lowest in the prison sample, and vary in ascending order between the factory, City Works and the College.

2   Remunerative power will be lowest in the voluntary organization. and the prison sample; and vary in descending order between the factory, City Works and the College.

3   Contingency based coercion will be highest in the prison sample, lowest in the voluntary organization and vary in descending order between the college, City Works and the factory.

4   Non-contingency coercion will be highest in the prison sample, lowest in the voluntary organization and vary in descending order between the college, City Works and the factory.

5   Involvement will be highest in the voluntary organization, lowest in the prison sample, and vary in ascending order between the factory, City Works, and the College.

6   Work alienation will be highest in the prison sample, lowest in the voluntary organization. and vary in descending order between the college, City Works and the factory.

Testing the essence of Etzioni's theory: a comparison between archetypal organizations

Table 1 shows a Oneway A.N.O.V.A. of power, involvement and work alienation amongst the lower participants of the three archetypal organizations. Almost all of the variables differ significantly by a substantial margin between organizations in the predicted direction. As expected, remunerative power does not vary significantly between the voluntary organization and the prison sample. Tukey's test is not significant for work alienation between the factory and the prison.

Comparing archetypal and intermediate organizations

Tables 2 and 3 show an extension of the previous analysis to all five research organizations.

With one exception, all differences in symbolic power are significant and in the predicted direction. The exception is between the voluntary organization and the college. Although symbolic power in the former is higher that in the latter, the difference is not significant.

The results for remunerative power show it is actually higher in the college than the factory, not the other way about as expected. The same applies to the comparison between City Works and the factory. The difference between the college and City Works is in the opposite to the predicted direction but is not significant.

Contingency based coercion differs significantly and in the predicted direction between the voluntary organization and the other four organizations, and between the prison and four other organizations. The difference between the college and the factory is significant but contingency based coercion is actually higher in the college. The difference between the college and City Works is not significant.

The results for non-contingency coercion exhibit a similar pattern in so far as it is significantly lower in the voluntary organization than the other four organizations and significantly higher in the prison sample than any of the other four groups. This does not apply to the three organizations in the middle of the spectrum where there are no significant differences in the level of non-contingency coercion.

As expected, involvement is significantly higher in the voluntary organization than any of the other organizations. It is also significantly lower in the prison than any of the others. Again this does not apply to the three organizations in the middle of the spectrum, there being no significant differences in involvement between the college, City Works and the factory. All pairwise contrasts for work alienation are significant with the exception the factory and prison (discussed earlier), and the college and City Works where the difference in means is negligible.

Table 1
One way A.N.O.V.A. of power, involvement and work alienation by organizational archetypes

ORGANIZATION (N=)	SYMBOLIC POWER	REMUNERATIVE POWER	C.B.C	N.C.C.	INVOLVEMENT	WORK ALIENATION
1. VOLUNTARY ORGANIZATION (32)	5.49	2.10	1.42	1.19	5.7	0.72
2. FACTORY (32)	3.10	3.07	3.38	1.99	4.0	2.84
3. PRISON (30)	2.08	2.22	6.06	4.32	1.64	3.53
F RATIO	51.01***	11.00***	151.00***	68.00***	107.00***	29.00***
TUKEY CONTRAST TEST	1>2* 1>3* 2>3*	1<2* 1<3* 2>3*	1<2* 1<3* 2<3*	1<2* 1<3* 2<3*	1>2* 1>3* 2>3*	1<2* 1<3* 2<3

Key to Abbreviations

C.B.C. Continengency based coercion   N.C.C.   Non-contingency coercion

*** p 0.001 ** p 0.01 * p < 0.05

Table 2
One way A.N.O.V.A. of power, involvement and work alienation by organization

ORGANIZATION (N=)	SYMBOLIC POWER	REMUNERATIVE POWER	C.B.C	N.C.C.	INVOLVEMENT	WORK ALIENATION
1. VOLUNTARY ORGANIZATION (32)	5.49	2.10	1.42	1.19	5.7	.72
2. COLLEGE (29)	5.12	4.39	4.40	2.5	4.14	1.86
3. CITY WORKS (41)	3.96	3.84	4.08	2.07	3.58	1.88
4. FACTORY (32)	3.10	3.07	3.38	1.99	4.00	2.84
5. PRISON (30)	2.08	2.22	6.06	4.32	1.64	3.53
F RATIO	33***	18***	81***	28***	50.74***	16.34***
TUKEY CONTRAST TEST	1>2	1<2*	1<2*	1<2*	1>2*	1<2*
	1>3*	1<3*	1<3*	1<3*	1>3*	1<3*
	1>4*	1<4*	1<4*	1<4*	1>4*	1<4*
	1>5*	1<5	1<5*	1<5*	1>5*	1<5*
	2>3*	2<3	2<3	2<3	2>3	2<3
	2>4*	2<4*	2<4*	2<4	2>4	2<4*
	2>5*	2>5*	2>5*	2<5*	2>5*	2<5*
	3>4*	3<4*	3<4*	3<4	3>4	3<4*
	3>5*	3>5*	3<5*	3<5*	3>5*	3<5*
	4>5*	4>5*	4<5*	4<5*	4>5*	4<5

*** p 0.001   ** p 0.01   * p < 0.05

C.B.C. Contingency based coercion.
N.C.C. Non-Contingency Coercion

142

Table 3
One way A.N.O.V.A. of power, involvement and work alienation by organization
(College lecturers as lower participants)

ORGANIZATION (N=)	SYMBOLIC POWER	REMUNERATIVE POWER	C.B.C	N.C.C.	INVOLVEMENT	WORK ALIENATION
1. VOLUNTARY ORGANIZATION (32)	5.49	2.10	1.42	1.19	5.7	0.72
2. COLLEGE (57)	4.16	3.57	2.9	1.83	4.85	1.19
3. CITY WORKS (41)	3.96	3.84	4.08	2.07	3.58	1.88
4. FACTORY (92)	3.10	3.07	3.38	1.99	4.00	2.84
5. PRISON (30)	2.08	2.22	6.06	4.32	1.64	3.53
F RATIO	26.00***	12.00***	80***	33.00***	58.00***	24.00***
TUKEY CONTRAST TEST	1>2*	1<2*	1<2*	1<2	1>2*	1<2
	1>3*	1<3*	1<3*	1<3*	1>3*	1<3*
	1>4*	1<4*	1<4*	1<4*	1>4*	1<4*
	1>5*	1<5	1<5*	1<5*	1>5*	1<5*
	2>3	2<3	2<3*	2<3	2>3	2<3
	2>4*	2<4	2<4	2<4	2>4	2<4*
	2>5*	2>5*	2<5*	2<5*	2>5*	2<5*
	3>4*	3>4*	3<4*	3<4	3>4	3<4*
	3>5*	3>5*	3<5*	3<5*	3>5*	3<5*
	4>5*	4>5*	4<5*	4<5*	4>5*	4<5

*** p 0.001   ** p 0.01   * p < 0.05

C.B.C. Contingency based coercion
N.B.C. Non-contingency coercion

143

College lecturers defined as lower participants

Since it could be argued that lecturing staff should be classified as the college's lower participants, a separate Oneway A.N.O.V.A was performed with this group representing the lower echelons.

Table 3 shows it makes very little difference to the overall pattern of results. Lecturers score lower on symbolic power than the blue collar staff of the college with the result that the difference between the voluntary organization. and the college is significant which was not the case in the previous analysis. However the difference between the college and City Works is narrowed and no longer significant.

Contingency based coercion is lower amongst college lecturers than blue collar staff in the two other employing organizations. The result is that all comparisons are significant with the exception of the college and the factory.

Although the mean is lower for lecturers than for blue collar staff, the results for non-contingency coercion are identical with the previous pattern. The exception is between the college and the voluntary organization. where, although the difference is in the predicted direction, it is not significant.

The pattern of results for involvement is unchanged. The same applies to work alienation with the exception of one comparison. The difference between the college and the voluntary organization still varies as predicted but is no longer significant.

Applying Etzioni's theory to intermediate organizations

In Table 4 total samples of the three employing organizations are compared with the voluntary organization, and prison sample. This shows some changes in pairs of contrasts but does not alter the pattern of results very much.

The difference between the voluntary organization. and the college on normative power is now significant whilst the difference between the college and City Works no longer is. The pattern of results for remunerative power is the same except that the difference between the college and City Works is no longer significant. The results for contingency based coercion reveal differences between all pairs of organizations in the hypothesised direction, with the exceptions of the factory and the college, and the factory and City Works. The pattern of results for non-contingency coercion is identical with the analysis applied to lower participants in Table 2. The same applies to involvement. There are still no significant differences between the three employing organizations. Indeed, the gap between means is almost negligible. Work alienation no longer differs significantly between the college and the voluntary organization, or the factory and City Works, otherwise the results are broadly similar to those shown in Table 2.

Sub analyses

The scale used to measure involvement is composed of three sub scales respectively, organizational identification, willingness to stay with the organization and willingness to exert effort. As no differences between the employing organizations had been observed on the combined scale, separate Oneway A.N.O.V.A.s were performed for each of the subscales to check whether there were any hidden differences between organizations on single components of involvement.

Only one significant difference was revealed; organizational identification was slightly higher in the college than City Works. The same analyses were performed for the lower participants of these three organizations but none of the differences were significant (not shown).

Table 4
One way A.N.O.V.A. of power, involvement and work alienation by total organization

ORGANIZATION (N=)	SYMBOLIC POWER	REMUNERATIVE POWER	C.B.C.	N.C.C.	INVOLVEMENT	WORK ALIENATION
1. VOLUNTARY ORGANISATION (32)	5.49	2.10	1.42	1.19	5.7	0.72
2. COLLEGE (148)	4.49	4.07	3.23	2.00	4.89	1.40
3. CITY WORKS (148)	4.35	4.16	3.77	2.03	4.67	1.82
4. FACTORY (146)	3.71	3.61	3.52	1.94	4.89	2.13
5. PRISON (32)	2.08	2.22	6.06	4.32	1.64	3.53
F RATIO	24***	22***	60***	30***	22***	17***
TUKEY CONTRAST TEST	1>2*	1<2*	1<2*	1<2*	1>2*	1<2
	1>3*	1<3*	1<3*	1<3*	1>3*	1<3*
	1>4*	1<4*	1<4*	1<4*	1>4*	1<4*
	1>5*	1<5	1<5*	1<5*	1>5*	1<5*
	2>3	2<3	2<3*	2<3	2>3	2<3
	2>4*	2>4	2<4	2<4	2>4	2<4*
	2>5*	2>5*	2<5*	2<5*	2>5*	2<5*
	3>4*	3>4*	3<4*	3<4	3>4	3<4
	3>5*	3>5*	3<5*	3<5*	3>5*	3<5*
	4>5*	4>5*	4<5*	4<5	4>5*	4<5*

*** p 0.001   ** p 0.01   * p < 0.05

C.B.C. Contingency based coercion
N.C.C. Non-contingency coercion

Testing hypotheses linking power, involvement and work alienation to organization level

Sub-hypotheses

1   Symbolic power will be highest for senior management, lowest for the lower participants and in between the two for middle management.

2   Remunerative power will be highest for lower participants, lowest for senior management and in between for middle management.

3   Contingency based coercion will be highest for lower participants, lowest for senior management and in between for middle management.

4   Non-contingency based coercion will be highest for lower participants, lowest for senior management and in between for middle management.

5   Involvement will be highest for senior management, lowest for the lower participants and in between the two for middle management.

6   Work alienation will be highest for lower participants, lowest for senior management and in between for middle management.

Each organization was analyzed separately. The lower participants group of the College and City Works included white collar clerical staff.

The college

Table 5 shows that senior management of the college were significantly less symbolically controlled than either the middle or lower ranks. Only one pair of groups differed significantly on remunerative power. This was significantly higher for senior than middle level staff. Contingency based coercion was significantly lower for senior staff than either middle or lower ranking participants. The F ratio's for involvement and work alienation were not significant.

Again, because college lecturers could theoretically be regarded as lower participants, separate Oneway A.N.O.V.A's were performed by extracting academic staff from the sample and grouping the into lower, middle and senior levels. There were no significant differences on any variable (not shown).

City Works

The only significant F ratios in City Works (See Table 6) were for Non-contingency coercion and involvement. Non-contingency coercion was higher for middle ranking staff than for lower participants. Senior staff scored considerably higher on involvement than lower participants.

The factory

Table 7 shows the results for the factory. Both symbolic and remunerative power were significantly higher for senior staff than either middle or lower echelons. The F ratios for both measures of coercion were not significant. Involvement and work alienation varied as predicted between both senior management and lower participants, and, middle management and lower participants.

Refining the analysis

Since many of the results did not accord with predictions, the analysis was refined to see whether differences might be more sharply pronounced between extremes within organizations. t-Tests on all variables were conducted between senior management and blue collar lower participants. (See Tables 8 A to 8 C).

In the College, symbolic power is substantially higher amongst the lower ranks. Contingency based coercion and involvement vary as predicted. No other comparisons are significant. Within City Works all comparisons are significant with the exception of contingency based coercion. Remunerative power in City Works is significantly higher for senior management than for blue collar staff. With the exception of contingency based coercion, all comparisons within the factory are significant and in the predicted direction.

Testing hypotheses linking power and involvement

Sub hypotheses

1   Symbolic power relates positively to involvement.

2   Remunerative power relates positively to involvement.

3   Contingency based coercion relates negatively to involvement.

4   Non-contingency coercion relates negatively to involvement.

Symbolic power and remunerative power correlate moderately in the employing organizations, (r's range 0.46*** to 0.52*** p≤ 0.001). Correlations pertaining to the other research

149

Table 6
One way A.N.O.V.A. of power, involvement and work alienation
by organizational level
(City works)

ORGANIZATION (N=)	SYMBOLIC POWER	REMUNERATIVE POWER	C.B.C.	N.C.C.	INVOLVEMENT	WORK ALIENATION
1. SENIOR (12)	5.19	4.91	3.42	1.25	5.66	1.08
2. MIDDLE (17)	4.51	4.32	3.94	2.45	4.77	1.53
3. LOWER (113)	4.23	4.05	3.78	2.05	4.44	1.95
F RATIO	2.23	1.86	0.67	3.63*	5.38	1.93
TUKEY CONTRAST TEST	1>2 1>3 2>3	1<2 1<3 2<3	1<2 1<3 2<3	1<2 1<3 2<3	1>2 1>3* 2>3	1<2* 1<3* 2<3

*** p < 0.001 level   ** p < 0.01 level   * p < 0.05 level

C.B.C. Contingency based coercion
N.C.C. Non-contingency coercion

Table 7
One way A.N.O.V.A. of power, involvement and work alienation by organization level
(Factory)

ORGANIZATION (N=)	SYMBOLIC POWER	REMUNERATIVE POWER	C.B.C.	N.C.C.	INVOLVEMENT	WORK ALIENATION
1. SENIOR (20)	5.04	4.43	3.7	1.46	5.22	0.60
2. MIDDLE (34)	4.59	4.60	3.81	2.09	5.45	1.11
3. LOWER (92)	3.10	3.07	3.38	1.99	4.0	2.84
F RATIO	19.77*	18.05***	1.97	1.9	7.01***	25.57***
TUKEY CONTRAST TEST	1>2* 1>3* 2>3*	1<2* 1<3* 2<3*	1<2 1<3 2<3	1<2 1<3 2<3	1>2 1>3 2>3	1<2* 1<3* 2<3

*** $p < 0.001$ level   ** $p < 0.01$ level   * $p < 0.05$ level

C.B.C. Contingency based coercion
N.C.C. Non-contingency coercion

153

Table 8 (a)
t-Test of power, involvement and work alienation by organization level
(Senior management and lower participants)
College

| | | SENIOR MANAGEMENT N=11 LOWER PARTICIPANTS N=29 | | | |
	MEAN	SD	T VALUE	DF	2 TAIL PROB
SYMBOLIC POWER	3.68 5.12	1.63 1.25	2.64	15	0.01
REMUNERATIVE POWER	3.93 4.39	1.55 1.73	0.82	20	NS
CONTINGENCY BASED COERCION	2.63 4.40	1.08 1.28	4.37	21	0.000
NON CONTINGENCY COERCION	2.32 2.5	1.11 1.63	0.40	27	NS
INVOLVEMENT	4.77 4.14	9.83 13.1	-2.24	24	0.03
WORK ALIENATION	1.36 1.86	1.72 1.07	1.12	30	NS

154

Table 8b
t-Test of power, involvement and work alienation by organization level (senior management and lower participants) City Works

	MEAN	SD	T VALUE	DF	2 TAIL PROB
	SENIOR MANAGEMENT N=12 LOWER PARTICIPANTS N=41				
SYMBOLIC POWER	5.19 3.96	1.52 1.73	-2.36	20	0.03
REMUNERATIVE POWER	4.91 3.84	0.97 1.47	-2.96	27	0.006
CONTINGENCY BASED COERCION	3.42 4.08	1.26 0.87	1.73	14	NS
NON CONTINGENCY COERCION	1.25 2.07	0.55 1.37	3.06	46	0.004
INVOLVEMENT	5.66 3.58	1.40 1.29	-3.29	19	0.004
WORK ALIENATION	1.08 1.88	1.55 1.40	1.71	20	0.002

155

Table 8c
t-Test of power, involvement and work alienation
by organization level
(senior management and lower participants)
Factory

	SENIOR MANAGEMENT N=20 LOWER PARTICIPANTS N=92				
	MEAN	SD	T VALUE	DF	2 TAIL PROB
SYMBOLIC POWER	5.04 3.10	1.29 1.60	-5.82	33	0.000
REMUNERATIVE POWER	4.43 3.07	1.34 1.42	-4.14	29	0.000
CONTINGENCY BASED COERCION	3.70 3.38	1.22 1.16	-1.09	27	NS
NON CONTINGENCY COERCION	1.46 1.99	0.72 1.19	2.61	45	0.01
INVOLVEMENT	5.22 4.00	12.72 4.7	-3.89	82	0.000
WORK ALIENATION	0.60 2.84	0.94 1.77	8.00	53	0.010

Table 9

Product moment correlations between power and involvement

(Lower participants)

	VOLUNTARY ORGANISATION (N=32)	COLLEGE (N=29)	CITY WORKS (N=41)	FACTORY (N=92)	PRISON (N=30)
SYMBOLIC POWER	0.57***	0.41*	0.47**	0.40**	0.59***
REMUNERATIVE POWER	0.18	0.52*	0.50**	0.21**	0.23*
CONTINGENCY BASED COERCION	0.06	0.17	-0.49**	0.07	-0.83***
NON-CONTINGENCY COERCION	0.03	-0.37*	-0.46**	-0.11	-0.49**

***p 0.001   ** p 0.01   *p 0.05

157

Table 10
Product moment correlations between power and involvement
(Full samples)

	VOLUNTARY ORGANISATION (N=32)	COLLEGE (N=158)	CITYWORKS (N=147)	FACTORY (N=146)	PRISON (N=32)
SYMBOLIC POWER	0.57***	0.29**	0.45**	0.42**	0.59**
REMUNERATIVE POWER	0.18	0.40**	0.41**	0.30**	0.23*
CONTINGENCY BASED COERCION	0.06	0.01	-0.14	0.08	-0.83***
NON-CONTINGENCY BASED COERCION	0.03	-0.27**	-0.25*	-0.14	-0.49**

***p 0.001   **p 0.01   * p 0.05

Relationship of involvement to other variables

Tables 11 and 12 show the correlation coefficients between involvement and other variables. Age tends to correlate moderately with involvement as does length of service though there are exceptions within the data. There appears to be almost no relationship between length of time in post grade (job level), closeness of supervision and involvement. Moderate to strong correlations are revealed between choice of work and involvement (range 0.29 to 0.69). Moderate to strong negative correlations (range -0.35 to 0.63) were revealed between work alienation and involvement with the exception of the voluntary organization where the result is not significant.

Table 11
Product moment correlations between involvement and other variables
(lower participants)

VARIABLES	VOLUNTARY ORGANISATIO (N=32)	COLLEGE (N=29)	CITY WORKS (N=41)	FACTORY (N=92)	PRISON (N=32)
AGE	0.11	0.46**	0.01	0.34	0.51**
LENGTH OF SERVICE /TIME SERVED	-0.30***	0.13	0.06	0.01	0.32***
LENGTH OF TIME IN POST GRADE	N/A	0.01	-0.4	-0.03	N/A
CLOSENESS OF SUPERVISION	N/A	0.17	0.14	0.17	N/A
CHOICE OF WORK	0.45**	0.29***	0.30***	0.32***	0.69***
WORK ALIENATION	-0.20	-0.55**	-0.63**	-0.43**	-0.35**

***p 0.001   ** p 0.01   * p 0.05

160

Table 12
Product moment correlations between involvement and other variables
(Full sample)

VARIABLES	WRVS (N=32)	COLLEGE (n=158)	CITY WORKS (n=142)	FACTORY (N=146)	PRISON (N=30)
AGE	0.11	0.30***	0.28***	0.27***	0.51**
LENGTH OF SERVICE /TIME SERVED	-0.30***	0.17***	0.26***	0.11	0.32***
LENGTH OF TIME IN POST GRADE	N/A	0.08*	-0.6	-0.06	N/A
CLOSENESS OF SUPERVISION	N/A	0.03	-0.05	0.01	N/A
CHOICE OF WORK	0.45**	0.30***	0.30*	0.32***	0.69***
WORK ALIENATION	-0.20	-0.50***	-0.54***	-0.51**	-0.35**

***p 0.001 ** p 0.01 * p 0.05

homogeneous with respect to size and development. Whilst this may serve as a control factor, it means, for example that no data are available on small businesses. It is possible that these might differ in their compliance structures given their size and workers' contact with decision makers.

It is also acknowledged that sample sizes for lower participants are fairly small. Further the data representing a coercive organization are not ideal, based as they are upon a convenience sample. It is appreciated that the analyses of power between organizations are based upon measures which are not absolutely identical. This means that the comparisons are approximate. Yet measurement cannot always be exact; arguably the use of appropriate, if slightly differing measures is a more valid test of a theory than one employing identical scales with inferior construct validity. In other words, as is often said in research, better an approximate answer to the right question than an exact answer to the wrong question.

Research aim 1: testing Etzioni's theory in relation to organizational archetypes

The first aim of the research was to assess the empirical validity of Etzioni's theory. Second, the study was intended to go beyond this and ascertain whether Etzioni's model of power and involvement combinations could be developed to achieve a more complex integrated statement based on the idea of systematic variation in power and involvement across the whole range of organizations.

For Etzioni's theory to be supported, the level of symbolic power in the voluntary organization should be higher than in the other two archetypal organizations, that is, the factory and the prison sample. Likewise there should be a higher level of coercion in the prison sample than the other two organizations, a high level of remunerative power within the factory, and systematic variation in the level of involvement between all three organizations. These relationships are clearly evident within the data. What is especially interesting is that the results show that power and work alienation as well as involvement relate systematically across the three organizations. In other words the data clearly support the idea of a more complex model, and demonstrate the role of work alienation as a new correlate.

It was suggested in Chapter One that possession of power resources does not necessarily mean that they will be used, but these results suggest they are utilised and in accordance with Etzioni's predictions. It is particularly interesting to see this in relation to coercion considering that was operationalised in this study as a mental rather than a physical phenomenon. This suggests there is scope to expand Etzioni's treatment of the concept as the presence of physical restrictions obviously has psychological ramifications.

The results for non-contingency coercion are particularly noteworthy. It was hypothesised this would vary systematically between organizations but the justification for this prediction was much weaker than for contingency based coercion. This is because non-contingency coercion concerns respondents' perceptions of injustice and it could be asked, whether those wielding power in utilitarian organizations should necessarily be more unfair than those in normative organizations. The data clearly indicate this to be so especially in prison sample where the level of non-contingency coercion is substantially higher than in either of the other two organizations.

One interpretation of these results is that they show the corrupting influence of power over those who wield it. That is, the availability of a high level of legitimate sanctions tempts power holders' to apply coercion arbitrarily. Another possibility is that the presence of high levels of legitimate coercion create feelings of fear and helplessness resulting in heightened feelings of persecution. This seems quite probable as the items of this scale relate to things like being blamed for something one has no control over and it was noted in the literature that feelings of powerlessness resulting from incarceration are common amongst inmates (e.g., Alpert, 1978). It is irrelevant whether prison warders use their power corruptly or not. It is clear from these results they are perceived as doing so. This qualifies the suggestion made earlier that performance related sanctions may be consistent with good management and promote morale. It seems that beyond a certain level, punishment creates feelings of helplessness and injustice.

It is worth noting that there is also a relationship between the nature of organizational membership and compliance structures. In a coercive organization membership is mandatory, in a utilitarian organization it may be semi voluntary and by definition, in a voluntary organization members have complete choice of whether to stay or go. This is synonymous with the concept of empowerment, that is, those in prison have comparatively little freedom over their lives, those in utilitarian and voluntary organizations have significantly more. There is evidence to suggest that empowerment and commitment are linked (Kushman, 1992). This relationship may also be adduced from the present study.

Research aim 2: a compliance continuum between intermediate organizations

Oneway A.N.O.V.A.'s were conducted between all five research organizations to test the hypotheses of systematic variation across a range of organizations which included examples of intermediate types. It is clear from the data that this idea can be applied between the voluntary organization, the prison sample and the employing organizations with isolated exceptions. The pattern is less consistent between the three employing organizations, the results seem to suggest that the relationship

166

applies for some variables and not others. All five organizations vary as predicted in respect of symbolic power with the exception of the voluntary organization and the college. Otherwise the evidence does not support the idea of a compliance continuum between intermediate organizations. This may be attributable to factors such as sample size or choice of organization. However taking into account the studies of Smith and Hepburn (1977) and Alpert (1978) reviewed in Chapter Three which found no evidence of a compliance continuum between maximum, medium and minimum security jails, it is possible that this aspect of Etzioni's theory is flawed.

Yet symbolic power varies between these three organizations exactly as predicted. Moreover the fact that organizational identification, a sub-scale of organization commitment, is significantly higher in the college than in City Works suggests that differences of degree in power and involvement as suggested by Etzioni may exist empirically. Conceivably although there is a broad relationship between power and involvement, involvement is determined by so many other variables that a small increase in the level of symbolic power does not automatically mean an increase in involvement. Another possibility is that involvement does actually vary between these organizations but the differences are too subtle to be detected by the research methodology.

It is interesting to note that remunerative power is significantly higher in the college than City Works or the factory when theoretically, the reverse may have been expected. Obviously it could be argued that the college should really be classified as a utilitarian organization and the difference is spurious. Nevertheless Etzioni clearly regards colleges as normative organizations and therefore as emphasising symbolic power. This result does not accord with the theory. One explanation could be that the items measuring remunerative power consist of a variety of rewards including pay increases, promotion and training. Factory operatives are paid a flat rate plus bonus; the prospects of increasing earnings through promotion and training are remote for the majority whereas in the college the potential for advancement for manual workers is a little better. Remunerative control depends on what resources the organization can afford to manipulate. These may be higher in a service organization than one which must compete in the market place.

The power to give also implies the power to take and this may explain why contingency based coercion is also higher in the college than the factory. Since the scale items concerning material rewards correspond closely with Etzioni's definition of remunerative power, the data highlight the need to re-examine the concept of remunerative power in employing organizations.

The role of the lower participants in defining the compliance structure of organizations

The evidence of the three employing organizations suggests that the lower participants do indeed determine the compliance structure of the organization. Comparisons between analyses based solely on the lower echelons and those based on full samples show that there are very few differences in the results. Furthermore it is evident that there are few significant differences between organizations at any other job level. Although this accords with Etzioni's predictions, the lack of any variation at middle levels is surprising none the less because middle management in the college consists of academic and administrative staff, whilst in the factory sample it is composed of chargehands and supervisors. Clearly control at middle and senior levels is determined by variables outside the scope of the study. In the case of senior management not least of these might be the personality and management style of the head of the organization. Another possibility is that non-supervisory staff become partly self supervising because of the need to set an example to others.

168

Defining the lower participants

It was expected that to regard lecturers as lower participants would sharpen the differences between the college and utilitarian organizations. This does not, however, appear to be the case. The most obvious explanation is that junior college lecturers perceive themselves, and are treated as, lower participants of the college academic hierarchy and this is reflected in control and involvement. That is, academic staff in basic grades do not see themselves as senior to clerical and administrative staff but view these groups as operating within a different compliance structure that has very little to do with them.

Research aim three: applying Etzioni's theory within organizations

This tested the hypothesis that the level of symbolic power and involvement increase with seniority whilst coercion decreases. The evidence is partial. The only significant differences revealed by the data are a substantial difference in symbolic power and involvement between the lower echelons and senior management of the factory.

When the analysis is refined to the comparison of extreme job levels, however, there are indications within the data of the possibility of such a relationship. One contra-indicator is that the lower participants in the college appear to be more normatively controlled than their senior colleagues. This is probably a reflection of the management style at the college's higher echelons as the results for the other two organizations are consistent with Etzioni's theory.

It is interesting to speculate what results might have been produced had senior management been defined in accordance with Parsons' (1960) institutional level. This would have entailed comparisons between the voluntary organization, a national body, perhaps a board of prison visitors; City Works Committee, the college governors and the factory board. It is conceivable that coercion might have been negligible at this level whilst scores on symbolic power and involvement soared above those for lower participants.

Yet does it matter? When Etzioni states that organizations require commitment to survive perhaps the question should be asked, 'commitment from whom?' Whose commitment is more important, those who produce, those who co-ordinate, those who formulate strategy or those at the institutional level linking organization and environment?

Research aim 4: work alienation as a new variable

The study also explored whether work alienation can be added as a new variable to Etzioni's model. In particular it sought to identify whether work alienation might vary systematically between organizations in a similar fashion to power and involvement. The evidence supports this hypothesis in that the data clearly show variations as predicted between organizational archetypes and, with the exception of the employing organizations, across the range of organizations. In short, work alienation varies in a similar way to the main study variables.

Before discussing the wider implications of these findings it is necessary to examine some of the details. The failure of the difference in work alienation between the factory employees and the ex-prisoners to reach statistical significance probably reflects the conservative element of Tukey's test. (The Mann Whitney test indicates the difference is significant (Drummond, 1989)). The margin of difference between the two scores is not great probably because work often relieves the monotony of prison life. The closeness of scores between the college and City Works suggests there is no difference in the level of work alienation between the two. This result is consistent with those

170

obtained for other comparisons between these two organizations. This suggests that either these two organizations are too close on the range for differences to show or, this aspect of the research model requires revision.

Overall the evidence strongly suggests work alienation is linked to compliance structures. It was noted earlier in this thesis that work alienation is associated with lack of intrinsic pride or meaning in work and tends to manifest itself where work fails to provide opportunities for the fulfilment of esteem needs. It was further noted that work alienation is often related to such factors as task characteristics, boredom, repetitiveness and deprivation of social contact (Kanungo, 1982). These results qualify this since arguably the tasks of volunteers in the voluntary organization, (making cups of tea, collecting and sorting clothing), are routine and repetitive yet alienation is lowest amongst this group. This suggests that need fulfilment depends not so much on the task itself, but for whom and for what reason it is performed.

The 'for whom' and 'for what' are dictated by the goal of the organization which in turn dictates its power structure. conceivably high commitment to the aims of the organization translates a potentially monotonous and menial task into a fulfilling one. Besides, job satisfaction a closely allied concept is a partly a product of autonomy and recognition (Hackman and Oldham, 1980). It seems reasonable to suggest that autonomy and recognition are higher in organizations such as the voluntary organization than in employing organizations, archetypal utilitarian ones especially. The converse is illustrated by the results for the prison sample which show work alienation is highest amongst those working in a coercive atmosphere even though some prison work such as metalwork, woodwork and academic study is potentially rewarding. This suggests that coercion destroys fulfilment. A subjective comment perhaps, but judging by conversations with some of the ex-inmates who completed questionnaires, such are the degradations experienced in prison, it would not be surprising if all pride is lost whilst incarcerated.

Relationship between power and involvement

Etzioni's theory assumes a relationship between power and involvement though Etzioni acknowledges that involvement is likely to be affected by many other variables besides power. The moderate correlations between symbolic power and involvement and remunerative power and involvement substantiate this. Further, correlations between involvement and other variables such as age and length of service demonstrate that involvement is indeed influenced by many variables besides power.

The weak and insignificant correlations between remunerative power and involvement in the voluntary organization and the prison sample. probably reflect the relatively low levels of remunerative power in each organization. The same applies to the correlation between contingency based coercion and involvement in the voluntary organization. It is not surprising that correlations between contingency based coercion and involvement within the employing organizations are negligible and insignificant. It was noted earlier that previous studies have recorded positive relationships, no relationships and weak to moderate negative relationships between contingency based coercion and various measures of employee satisfaction (e.g.,Podsakoff, 1982; Podsakoff et al., 1982). However, previous studies have all been of employing organizations and it is striking that the prison sample reveals a strong negative correlation ($r = -0.83$ $p<0.001$) between contingency based coercion and involvement. This result seems to imply that the relationship between coercion and involvement is not linear; possibly the impact of coercion is only felt once it reaches a certain level. Another possibility is that as suggested earlier, perhaps above a certain level, contingency sanctions are no longer perceived as related to behaviour, hence their markedly depressing effect upon involvement.

Overall the results suggest that non-contingency coercion has a more depressing effect upon involvement than contingency based coercion presumably because of its arbitrary nature which engenders feelings of powerlessness. The result for the voluntary organization is probably not statistically significant because the mean is extremely low. Non-contingency coercion is higher within the employing organizations which is probably reflected in the moderate negative correlations for the college and City Works. It is difficult to explain why the correlation for the factory blue collar sample is weak and insignificant. Perhaps the nature of production work with emphasis on quality control and very specific and clearly communicated standards of hygiene and timekeeping removes discretionary power from supervisors. The negative correlation between non-contingency coercion and involvement is substantially higher ($r = -0.49$ $p<0.01$) in the prison sample than any of the other organizations. This may suggest that like contingency based coercion, above a certain level, non-contingency coercion has a markedly depressing effect upon involvement.

Relationship between involvement and other variables

The findings of the present study augment existing studies of organizational commitment. The results of the present study are consistent with previous findings with the exception of tenure (Mathieu and Zajac, 1990). For example, as expected, age tends to be moderately correlated with involvement. The negligible and insignificant correlations within the voluntary organization and City Works (lower participants) probably reflect the relatively narrow age ranges of these groups. The voluntary organization sample contains a high proportion of older members. This is also true of City Works, although the mean age and age range are comparable with other samples, the mode is only twenty-four which may be why the correlation coefficient is negligible and not significant. Whereas within the literature tenure (length of service) is related to involvement, correlations for blue collar lower participants are negligible and insignificant. This is probably because involvement is associated with career development which is less relevant to blue collar workers than other groups of staff.

There were also indications in the literature of a relationship between length of time on a certain pay grade and commitment. The results do not substantiate this. There could be many reasons why, the main one being that promotion is not a particularly important issue amongst blue collar staff. Expectations amongst white collar and professional staff might be lower than their American counterparts. This research was conducted at a time of economic recession when the three employing organizations were contracting and there may have been a feeling amongst staff that they were fortunate just to be in employment. On the whole however the parallels between these results and those of American studies support Luthan's et al.'s, (1985) conclusion that commitment is not culture specific.

Work alienation and involvement are consistently moderately correlated. This accords with studies reviewed in earlier chapters which found links between organization commitment and various measures of employee satisfaction (e.g., Vandenberg and Lance, 1992). The unresolved question is whether commitment causes satisfaction or, whether satisfaction is a precursor of commitment, or, whether satisfaction and commitment are both determined by a third and as yet unidentified variable.

Although this research was not designed as a causal study, the evidence of inter-relations between power, involvement and work alienation provide empirical support for the argument presented in Chapter Five. That is, if the goals of the organization

174

determine the nature of the task which in turn determines the power structure, then it is fruitless to look towards either involvement as determining satisfaction (or in this case work alienation) or vice versa. Power precedes both in the chain of causality.

Inter-correlations between power measures

As expected, symbolic and remunerative power are intercorrelated in the three employing organizations. It could be argued that the measures are insufficiently discriminating but this seems unlikely as there is clearly no relationship between the two within the voluntary organization. and the prison sample where there are virtually no material rewards. It seems more probable that where symbolic and remunerative power co-exist in significant amounts, they tend to be perceived in concert. Spekman (1979) in trying to operationalise French and Raven's typology noted as had researchers before him, that non-coercive powers tended to be applied in concert. Similarly, Ornstein (1986) observed that reward and empathic symbols are processed simultaneously. In other words, to reward someone materially simultaneously symbolises approval.

Rewards and coercion were expected to relate negatively. The low to moderate positive correlations observed within employing organizations suggest that the exercise of control involves both reward and punishment. In other words, conscientious managers who reward staff and pay attention to them are also careful to impose order. This is partly a reflection of the way in which coercion was operationalised, had it been measured as a physical phenomenon then it is less likely that rewards and punishments would have been positively correlated.

Relevance of results to related areas

Finally it is necessary to consider these results from the standpoint of research into rewards and punishment and research into organizational commitment. Whereas previous studies have concentrated on the impact of personal and role related factors these results clearly demonstrate that supervisory reward and punishment behaviour and commitment are affected by structural factors. Moreover they show that rewards, punishments, involvement, work alienation and commitment are all interrelated. Taking the findings of this research with those of previous studies, they indicate the need for a certain amount of conceptual integration.

Summary

In this chapter the results of the research were discussed. The purpose of the discussion was to summarise the data, to identify patterns therein and to highlight findings of particular significance. It was suggested that the most conclusive evidence pertains to power, involvement and work alienation between archetypal examples of each of Etzioni's three types of organization. The next most conclusive area concerns comparisons between all five organizations though the results pertaining to the factory, college and City Works are equivocal. There is some evidence to suggest the possibility of systematic variation by organization level. In the next chapter the evidence is weighed and conclusions are drawn as to the extent to which findings support the research model.

11 Conclusions

Introduction

The purpose of this closing chapter is to state the study conclusions and to discuss their theoretical and empirical implications. The research problem was basically two fold, to examine the empirical validity of Etzioni's basic theory and to test whether, and how far, this could be developed into a more complex model.

Etzioni's basic theory was summarised as consisting of a taxonomy of congruent compliance patterns. The research model, based partly on the literature and partly on logic, proposed the idea of a spectrum of compliance structures and hypothesised systematic interrelations between power and involvement plus work alienation as a new correlate.

This study suggests three things. First it provides evidence in support of Etzioni's basis theory. Second it has shown how the explanatory power of the theory can be improved by demonstrating the validity of a more complex model. Third it has shown the value of linking ideas from different disciplines, that is, supervisory reward and punishment behaviours and organization commitment.

The empirical validity of the research model

Power, involvement and work alienation in archetypal coercive, utilitarian and normative organizations

Testing of Etzioni's basic theory evolved round the hypotheses that power and involvement vary systematically between organizations according to whether they are normative, utilitarian or coercive. The results clearly show that relatively speaking, coercive organizations rely more on coercive power than any other type. Likewise utilitarian and normative organizations also rely heavily upon remunerative and symbolic power respectively. As predicted, involvement in the coercive organization is low, high in the normative organization and in between in the utilitarian organization. It is concluded therefore that the evidence substantiates Etzioni's theory.

It is also clear that the idea of a compliance continuum between organizational archetypes is soundly based. The results show that not only do power and involvement vary from high to low (or vice versa) across the spectrum of organizations but that the hypotheses were also supported for work alienation. This adds to Etzioni's theory in that as it shows that it can be regarded as a theory of power, involvement and work alienation. Moreover it demonstrates that it is possible to expand the theory to explain not only the predominant power, but to state how other forms of power vary concomitantly in each of the archetypal organizations. In its original form, Etzioni's theory simply predicted which kind of power each of the three types of organizations would rely upon. This study provides evidence as to the relative usage of the two other power bases within each type of organization, and relative to the other two. This theoretical development is best illustrated by a recapitulation of earlier figures:

	INVOLVEMENT		
POWER	LOW (ALIENATIVE)	MEDIUM (CALCULATIVE)	HIGH (MORAL)
COERCIVE	X	0	X
REMUNERATIVE	0	X	0
NORMATIVE	0	0	X

Key: X = congruent power and involvement combinations.
        O = incongruent power and involvement combinations.

Figure 5 Etzioni's power and involvement combinations

	ORGANIZATION		
	COERCIVE	UTILITARIAN	NORMATIVE
SYMBOLIC POWER	Low	Medium	High
REMUNERATIV POWER	Low	High	Low
COERCION	High	Medium	Low
INVOLVEMENT	Low	Medium	High
WORK ALIENATION	High	Medium	Low

Figure 6 The research model as substantiated by the data

Figure 5 shows Etzioni's theory expressed as a set of power and involvement combinations. Figure 6 shows the development of Etzioni's theory towards a spectral and interrelated model with work alienation as a new correlate. The evidence clearly substantiates this model.

Relations between power, involvement and work alienation in intermediate organizations

The evidence concerning this aspect of the research is equivocal. It was expected that there would be systematic variation on all variables between all five research organizations. Indeed there are many significant pairwise contrasts within the data between the prison, the voluntary organization and the intermediate organizations, and also numerous significant results between the three employing organizations (notably for symbolic power). Against this however must be weighed that there are gaps in the data between the three employing organizations especially regarding systematic variations in the level of involvement.

The question is, do these results mean that the proverbial bottle is half full or half empty? The contrasts between the voluntary organization, the prison, and intermediate organizations may only be confirmation of the latter's status as utilitarian or borderline utilitarian/normative organizations in which case the idea of a compliance continuum between organizations is hard to accept. Yet nearly all comparisons between the voluntary organization and the college are significant. This could be interpreted as an important indicator of the applicability of the theory to a whole range of organizations.

It is concluded then that the data provide partial support for the concept of intermediate organizations where these are relatively far apart on the spectrum as was the case between the college and the voluntary organization. However, the whole issue of compliance relations between employing organizations be they utilitarian or normative requires further investigation. Whilst this research provides at most qualified support, equally there are too many positive indications within the data to dismiss the idea of intermediate organizations.

The relevance of Etzioni's theory to compliance structures within organizations

The evidence concerning compliance relations within organizations is likewise equivocal. Little support exists for the idea of fine gradations in power and involvement as suggested by Etzioni. The prediction does however hold good between senior management and lower participants in two of the three research organizations. Again it is concluded that there are too many positive indications within the data to reject the idea. The data qualify Etzioni's theory by showing that where such contrasts exist, they are most likely to be found between extreme hierarchial levels.

The relationship between power and involvement

It is concluded that the data broadly support Etzioni's theory. Normative and remunerative power correlate positively with involvement though in the case of the latter, the correlations are weaker. This is consistent with Etzioni's prediction that normative power is conducive to high involvement. Further, it is concluded that beyond a certain level, both forms of coercion depress involvement.

Implications for related fields

The research findings are relevant to the literature on supervisor rewards and punishment behaviour and also to the literature on organizational commitment. They show that both variables are affected by organization goals and that they may vary by organization level. Research into supervisory reward and punishment behaviour has so far been concerned with the impact of these on various measures of satisfaction and the motivational determinants of supervisors' propensity to reward or punish. Such studies have concluded that supervisors were more likely to respond punitively where inadequate performance was attributed to poor attitude than to ineptitude. This links with Etzioni's idea that power is determined by the subject's motivation to comply. The difference is that Etzioni takes this a stage further and relates compliance with the goals of the organization.

Research on organizational commitment has concentrated on examining the effects of various situational and personal variables, according to Mathieu and Zajac (1990) without identifying any theoretical reason why the various antecedents and correlates are potentially relevant. This study demonstrates that an organization's mission is a possible determinant of commitment. Moreover, this conclusion is based on a theoretical rationale.

Theoretical and empirical implications and suggestions for further research

The present study suggests several ideas for further research. The most obvious of these is that more studies of the basic model are required incorporating a larger number of organizations utilising a variety of methodologies. In particular, it would be interesting to compare these results with interview data and observation. These methods are more capable of capturing the subtleties and intricacies of power relations and their effects upon involvement. They are also more capable of a deeper examination of what it means to be involved, apathetic or hostile.

Some theoretical bridge building seems appropriate such as examination of the relationship (if any) between selection of power tactics such as knowledge and influence, to formal compliance structures. Likewise there is a clearly a case for examining the concept of multiple involvements (Reichers, 1985) in the context of Etzioni's theory. If work involvement or work alienation in the context of the present study are to linked to compliance structures so might be involvement in the work group and other aspects of the immediate organization.

In defence of researching common sense

Arguably it is hardly surprising that normative power is higher in the voluntary organization than in the prison sample. Quite apart from the fact that many apparently common sense hypotheses have yet to be substantiated empirically, (e.g., the link between job satisfaction and performance (Fisher, 1980; and commitment and performance, (Randall, 1990)), this is hardly important aspect of the research. Much more significant is the fact that researching intuitive hypotheses may reveal unsuspected results.

One curious finding of the present study is the level of symbolic power amongst the prison sample. Whilst this is indeed significantly lower than in the other organizations what is striking is that the mean of 2.08 is far from negligible. This observation becomes all the more significant when considered in conjunction with the correlation of 0.59^{***} ($p \leq 0.001$) between symbolic power and involvement. A similar observation can be made for remunerative power where the mean is 2.22 and the correlation with involvement is 0.23^{*} ($p \leq 0.05$). Both variables correlate despite the comparatively lower mean level of involvement of 1.64.

The data suggests two things. First that coercive organizations clearly rely to some extent upon praise, recognition and other forms of rewards. Second that even where mingled with high levels of coercion, rewards, symbolic ones especially, have a marked effect upon commitment. Indeed it was noted in Chapter Three that there is evidence which suggests that total reliance upon coercion in a prison environment is potentially de-stabilising (Hepburn, 1985; Stojkovik, 1986). What is unclear and a potential issue for further research is the interaction between coercion and symbolic reward. Moreover why does it have such a striking effect upon commitment? Is it because praise, recognition and so forth reduce feelings of powerlessness by showing inmates that they can gain at least some control over their experience of incarceration?

A further question which cannot be answered by the present study is why contingency based coercion should have a markedly more depressing effect upon involvement than non-contingency based coercion in the prison sample. We need to develop our understanding of the interaction between both forms of power. Another issue is the comparatively high level of non-contingency coercion in City Works. What situations give rise to such arbitrary use of power?

A reconceptualization of Etzioni's theory

The least empirically substantiated aspect of Etzioni's theory is that of fine gradations of power and involvement between extreme and mild examples of each of the three archetypes. A more promising field of enquiry is the link between powerlessness and alienation (e.g., Alpert, 1978 ; Smith and Hepburn, 1977) and conversely between empowerment and involvement (Kushman, 1992). A basic hypotheses for testing might be that involvement varies concomitantly with empowerment. Such an approach might pave the way towards the identification and classification of different types of utilitarian organization and so forth.

The subtleties of power and involvement

The present study reflects the linear nature of Etzioni's theory. It seems reasonable to suggest, however, that qualitative as well as quantitative differences exist in power and involvement in organizations. This applies with particular force to compliance relations within organizations. Senior managers may escape censure for being late but may be kept in check by fear of losing power and status as a result of organizational re-structuring or some such device.

Etzioni stresses the positive aspects of symbolic and remunerative power. What of their negative dimensions? The findings of the present study and accompanying review of the literature show that the relationship between sanctions based on remunerative power (contingency based punishment) is not fully understood. For example, under what conditions are high levels of positive and negative re-enforcement likely to be found? Less still is known about the use and impact of negative forms of symbolic power. Such issues require investigation if the workings of power and involvement are to be elucidated.

An issue not addressed by the present study is organizational sub-groupings. Etzioni suggests that these too vary systematically. For example, research and development professionals might be more normatively controlled than production managers by virtue of their relative freedom from numerical targets and so forth. It is interesting to speculate on the potential extent of such distinctions. Studies of organization culture have detected differences between groups working within yards of one another upon the same factory floor and within work groups (e,g., Ackroyd, 1990). How far, for example, does the informal organization mirror the formal organization?

Power and involvement in and around organizations of the future

Control in organizations as Littler and Salaman (1982) remind us is but a means to an end. The end remains compliance. The genesis of advanced manufacturing techniques, emphasis upon quality standards and the development of ever more sophisticated information technology appears set to create drastic changes in the management of organizations. Not least of these is likely to be a move towards individual self-regulation and autonomous work groups in place of conventional and non-value adding supervisory and managerial functions. Such developments place a new emphasis upon employee involvement in areas traditionally the prerogative of management (Drummond and Chell, 1992). One of the future paradoxes of organization is the freedom afforded by self-regulation and compliance with quality standards as the organizational imperative. How will organizations seek to reconcile the two in order to obtain compliance? What are the implications of 'flat' organizations (Handy, 1990) for power relations and employee involvement?

The new emphasis upon inter-departmental integration and cooperation will place a premium upon compliance relations between organizational sub-groups. Whilst the 'total quality management literature,' may stress the need for cooperative relations how do these square with the realities of power in organizations?

The proliferation of sub-contracting will require researchers to look beyond the organization as the unit of analysis (Clegg, 1992). A critical dimension of organization will be the customer/supplier chain. For instance, how far will an organization's relations with its suppliers reflect the former's compliance structure or vice versa? What will be the relationship between congruence and effectiveness? Deming (1986) has argued that the ideal relationship is one akin to the normative archetype, that is, based upon mutual trust, understanding and cooperation. In practice, in many organizations including leading Japanese manufacturers control appears to be coercive, based upon market forces (Drummond, 1992,b). Will this always be the case or will suppliers form self-protective organizations akin perhaps to medieval guilds which in addition to protecting trade monopoly also discharged an important social function? If this happens, how will such organizations combined utilitarian and normative goals be reconciled? As Etzioni (1975) observes, it is the aytypical and incongruent organizations which are potentially the most fruitful subjects for research. Postmodern society promises to open up a wealth of opportunities for new directions in research.

APPENDICES

Appendix 1
Sampling percentages

		COLLEGE	CITY WORKS	FACTORY
SENIOR MANAGEMENT	n= SS= %=	16 16 (100%)	18 18 (100%)	24 24 (100%)
MIDDLE MANAGEMENT	n= SS= %=	404 120 (30%)	46 46 (100%)	120 60 (50%)
WHITE COLLAR LOWER PARTICIPANTS	n= SS= %=	191 60 (31%)	116 116 (100%)	---------
BLUE COLLAR LOWER PARTICIPANTS	n= SS= %=	300 100 (33%)	380 130 (34%)	900 120 (13%)

Code: 'n =' denotes approximate number within each stratum
         'SS' denotes number sampled
         '%' denotes percentage sampled in each stratum

191

Appendix 2
Items used to measure power

1   Your immediate supervisor would personally pay you a compliment if you did outstanding work.

2   You would receive a reprimand for your supervisor if you were late in coming to work.

3   Your supervisor would recommend that you should be dismissed if you were absent for several days without notifying the organisation of a resonable excuse.

4   Your supervisor would see that you will eventaully go as far as you would like in this organization if your work in consistently above average.

5   Your supervisor frequently holds you accountable for things that you have not control over.

6   Your supervisor would get onto yo if you work was not as good as the work of others in your department.

7   Your supervisor would recommend that you be promoted if you work was better than others who were otherwise equally qualified.

8   Your supervisor is often displeased with your work for no apparent reason.

9   Your supervisor would tell his\her boss if your work was outstanding

Appendix 3
Adaptation of power items for the use with ex-inmates

1   The warders would personally pay you a compliment if your behaviour was outstanding.

2   You would receive a reprimand from the warders if you broke the rules.

3   The warders would recommend that you loose remission if you misbehaved.

4   The warders would see that you got a cushy job if your behaviour was good.

5   The warders frequently blamed you for things that weren't your fault.

6   The warders would get onto you if your behaviour was not as good as other prisoners.

7   The warders could make life easy for you if you were well behaved.

8   The warders were often displeased with your for no apparent reason.

9   The warders would give a good report if you behaviour was outstandingly good.

10   The warders would recommend that you get no privileges if your behaviour was below standard.

11   The warders would put you on report if your behaviour was consistently below acceptable standards.

12   The warders would make you a trusty if you were well
      behaved.

13   The warders were often critical of you even when you
      behaved well.

14   The warders would give you special recognition if your
      behaviour was especially good.

15   The warders would recommend that you did not receive
      privileges or special consideration if your behaviour
      was only average.

16   The warders would encourage you to do further
      training or give your other help if it would help you on
      release.

17   You were frequently reprimanded by warders without
      knowing why

18   The warders' reports of your behaviour would be in
      agreement with your views of your behaviour.

Appendix 4a
Means and standard deviations of measurement variables
(lower participants of each organization)

	VOLUNTARY ORGANISATION (N=32)	CITY WORKS (N=41)	COLLEGE (N=29)	FACTORY (N=92)	PRISON SAMPLE (N=30)
SYMBOLIC POWER					
mean	5.49	4.11	3.34	3.10	2.08
sd	1.08	1.47	1.03	1.60	0.93
REMUNERATIVE POWER					
mean	2.10	4.40	3.84	3.07	2.22
sd	0.54	1.73	1.47	1.42	0.84
CONTINGENCY BASED COERCION					
mean	1.42	4.36	4.08	3.38	6.06
sd	0.48	1.28	1.22	1.16	1.15
NON-CONTINGENCY BASED COERCION					
mean	1.19	2.59	2.06	1.99	4.32
sd	0.42	1.63	1.20	1.19	1.37
INVOLVEMENT					
mean	5.7	4.14	3.58	4.00	1.64
sd	0.52	1.41	1.26	1.42	0.82
WORK ALIENATION					
mean	0.72	1.86	1.88	2.84	3.53
sd	0.71	1.72	1.55	1.77	1.59

Appendix 4b
Means and standard deviations of measurement variables
(employing organizations, full samples)

	CITY WORKS (N=142)	COLLEGE (N=158)	FACTORY (N=146)
SYMBOLIC POWER			
mean	4.35	4.49	3.71
sd	1.55	1.55	1.75
REMUNERATIVE POWER			
mean	4.16	4.07	3.61
sd	1.52	1.68	1.58
CONTINGENCY BASED COERCION			
mean	3.77	3.23	3.52
sd	1.23	1.33	1.19
NON-CONTINGENCY BASED COERCION			
mean	2.03	2.00	1.94
sd	1.22	1.26	1.23
INVOLVEMENT			
mean	4.67	4.89	4.89
sd	1.27	1.24	1.29
WORK ALIENATION			
mean	1.82	1.40	2.13
sd	1.60	1.35	1.83

Means and standard deviations of
measurement variables
(by organization level)

	COLLEGE			CITY WORKS			FACTORY		
LEVEL (N=)	1 (65)	2 (82)	3 (11)	1 (113)	2 (17)	3 (12)	1 (92)	2 (34)	3 (20)
SYMBOLIC POWER									
mean	4.93	4.25	3.68	4.23	4.51	5.18	3.1	4.59	5.06
sd	1.40	1.57	1.63	1.57	1.30	1.51	1.6	1.58	1.29
REMUNERATIVE POWER									
mean	4.51	3.72	3.93	4.08	4.32	4.91	3.07	4.60	4.60
sd	1.74	1.57	1.55	1.52	1.70	0.97	1.41	1.48	1.34
CONTINGENCY BASED COERCION									
mean	3.78	2.87	2.63	3.78	3.94	3.41	3.38	3.81	3.7
sd	1.37	1.16	1.08	1.22	1.21	1.26	1.16	1.22	1.22
NON-CONTINGENCY BASED COERCION									
mean	2.07	1.89	2.32	2.05	2.45	1.25	1.99	2.09	1.46
sd	1.38	1.17	1.11	1.22	1.34	0.85	1.19	1.48	0.72
INVOLVEMENT									
mean	4.78	4.89	5.44	4.44	4.78	5.67	4.56	5.44	5.33
sd	1.36	1.14	1.09	1.26	0.97	1.30	1.41	0.98	0.53
WORK ALIENATION									
mean	1.63	1.21	1.36	1.94	1.53	1.08	2.84	1.12	0.6
sd	1.51	1.25	1.03	1.61	1.54	1.38	1.77	1.30	0.94

Level 1 denotes lower participants
Level 2 denotes middle management
Level 3 denotes senior management

Appendix 5
Reliability estimates for each measurement scale

SCALE	ORGANIZATION	ALPHA
Normative Power Sub Scale (4 Items)	Voluntary Organization	0.80
	College	0.76
	City Works	0.82
	Factory	0.77
	Prison Sample	0.79
Renumerative Power Sub Scale (4 Items)	Voluntary Organization	0.65
	College	0.79
	City Works	0.78
	Factory	0.71
	Prison Sample	0.76
Work Alienation (5 Items)	Voluntary Organization	0.71
	College	0.72
	City Works	0.77
	Factory	0.84
	Prison Sample	0.77
Contingency Based Coercion (6 Items)	Voluntary Organization	0.78
	College	0.75
	City Works	0.67
	Factory	0.53
	Prison Sample	0.94
Non Contingency Based Coercion (4 Items)	Voluntary Organization	0.77
	College	0.77
	City Works	0.68
	Factory	0.66
	Prison Sample	0.86
Involvement	Voluntary Organization	0.63
	College	0.84
	City Works	0.82
	Factory	0.80
	Prison Sample	0.88

Bibliography

Ackroyd, S. and Crowdy, P. A. (1990), 'Can culture be managed? Working with raw material: the case of English slaughtermen', *Personnel Review*, 19(5), pp.3- 13.

Adler, P. A. and Adler, P. (1988), 'Intense loyalty in organizations: a case study of college athletics', *Administrative Science Quarterly*, 33, pp.401-417.

Adams, J. D. Hayes, J. and Hopson, B, (1976), (Transition:) *Understanding and Managing Personal Change*, Martin Robertson, London. (1975).

Adams, J. S. 'Inequity in social exchange', In L. Berkowitz (Ed) *Advances in Experimental Psychology*, 2, Academic Press, New York. (1965).

Allen, N. J. and Mayer, J. P. (1990), 'The measurement and antecedents of affective, continuance and normative commitment to the organization', *Journal of Occupational Psychology*, 63, pp.1-18.

Allutto, J. A., Hrebiniak, L. G. and Alonsi, R. (1973), 'On operationalising the concept of commitment', *Social Forces*, 51, pp.448-454.

Alpert, G. P. (1978), 'Prisons as formal organizations - compliance theory in action', *Sociology and Social Research*, 63 (1), pp.112-130.

Angle, H. L. and Perry, J. L. (1981), 'An empirical assessment of organizational commitment and organizational effectiveness',

Administrative Science Quarterly,   26, pp.1-14.

Angle, H. L. and Perry, J. L. (1986), 'Dual commitment and labour management relationship climates', *Academy of Management Journal*, 29(1), pp.31-50.

Argyris, C. *(1964), Integrating the Individual and the Organization*, John Wiley, New York.

Arvey, R. D. and Ivancevich, J. M. (1980), 'Punishment in organizations: A review, propositions and research suggestions', *Academy of Management Review*, 5 (1), pp.123-132.

Arvey, R. D. Davis, G. A. and Nelson, S. M. (1984), 'Use of discipline in an organization: A field study', *Journal of Applied Psychology*, 69 (1), pp.448-460.

Arvey, R. D. and Jones, A. P. (1985), 'The use of discipline in orsettings: a framework for future research', In L. L. Cummins, and B. M. Staw. (Eds), *Research in Organizational Behaviour. Vol,7*, JAI Press, London.

Assad, T. (1987), 'On ritual and discipline in medieval Christian monasticism', *Economy and Society*, 16(2), pp.159-203.

Astley, W. G. and Sachdeva, P. S. (1984), 'Structural sources, of intraorganizational power: A theoretical synthesis' *Academy of Management Review*, 9(1), pp.104-113.

Attewell, P. and Gernstein, D. R. (1979), 'Government policy and local practice', *American Sociological Review*, 44, pp.311-327.

Bacharach, P. and Baratz, M. S. *(1970), Power and Poverty: Theory and Practice*, New York: Oxford Press.

Bacharach, S. B. and Lawler, E. J. *(1980), Power and Politics in Organizations*, Jossey Bass, San Fransisco.

Baker, A. J. (1982), 'The problem of authority in radical movement groups. A case   study of lesbian feminist organization', *Journal of Applied Behaviour*, 18(3), pp.323-341.

Barling, J. Wade, B. and Fullager. C. (1992), 'Predicting, employee commitment to company and union: divergent models', *Journal of Occupational Psychology,*   63, pp.49-61.

Bateman, T. S. (1986), 'The escalation of commitment in sequential decision making: Situational and personal moderators and limiting conditions', *Decision Sciences*, 17(1) pp.33-49.

Bateman, T. S. and Strasser, S. (1984), 'A longitudinal analysis of the antecedents of organizational commitment', *Academy of Management Journal*, 27(1), pp.93-112.

Bar-Hayim, A. and Berman, G. S. (1992), 'The dimmensions of organizational commitment', *Journal of Organizational Behavior*, 13, pp.379-387.

Beauman, K. B. (1977), *Green Sleeves*, Seely Service, London.

Becker, E. (1975), *Escape from Evil*, Collier MacMillan, London.

Becker, H. S. (1960), 'Notes on the concept of commitment', *American Journal of Sociology*, 66, pp.32-40.

Becker, T. E. (1992), 'Foci and bases of commitment: are they distinctions worth making'? *Academy of Management Journal*, 35(1), pp.232-244.

Bettelheim, B. (1943), 'Individual and mass behaviour in extreme situations', *Journal of Abnormal and Social Psychology*, 38, pp.417-452.

Beyer, J. M. and Trice, H. M. (1984), 'A field study on the use and perceived effects of discipline in controlling work performance', *Academy of Management Journal*, 27(4), pp.743-764.

Bierstedt, R. (1950), 'An analysis of social power', *American Sociological Review*, 13(6), pp.730-738.

Bigelow, P. H. and Driscoll, R. H. (1973), 'Effect of minimizing coercion on rehabilitation of offenders', *Journal of Applied Psychology*, 57(1), pp.10-14.

Blau, P. M. and Scott, R. W. (1963), *Formal Organizations: A Comparative Approach*, Routledge and Ill Kegan Paul, London.

Blauner, R. (1964), *Alienation and Freedom*, III, Chicago.

Bloch, H. A. (1947), 'The personality of inmates of concentration camps', *American Journal of Sociology*, 52, pp.335-41.

Boettcher, R. E. (1973), 'Test of Etzioni Compliance Theory in a public welfare system', *Public Welfare*, 31(3), pp.43-49.

Bluedorn, A. C. (1982), 'A unified model of turnover from organizations', *Human Relations*, 35, pp.135-153.

Bowers, D. G. and Seashore, S. E. (1966), 'Predicting organizational effectiveness with a four factor theory of leadership', *Administrative Science Quarterly*, 11, pp.238-263.

Boyle, J. (1973), *A Sense of Freedom*, Pan Books, Harmondsworth.

Brockner, J. Tyler, T. R. and Cooper-Schneider, R. (1992), 'The influence of prior commitment to an institution on reactions to perceived unfairness: the higher they are, the harder they fall', *Administrative Science Quarterly*, 37, pp.241-261.

Brown, M. E. (1969), 'Identification and some conditions of organizational involvement', *Administrative Science Quarterly*, 14, pp.346-355.

Brown, W. (1971), *Organization*, Heineman, London.

Buchanan, B. (1974), 'Building organizational commitment: The socialization of managers in work organizations', *Administrative Science Quarterly*, 19, pp.533-546.

Burns, L. R, Andersen, R. M. and Shortell, S. M. (1990), 'The effect of hospital control strategies on physician satisfaction and physician-hospital conflict', *Health Service Review*, 25(3), pp.527-560.

Cheeny, G. (1983), 'On the various and changing means of organizational membership - a field study of organizational identification', *Communication Monographs*, 50(4), pp.342-362.

Chell, E. (1985), *Participation and Organization: A Social Psychological Approach*, MacMillan, London.

Child, J. (1984), *Organization: A Guide to Problems and Practice*, Harper and Row, London.

Chow, E. N. L. and Grusky, O. (1980), 'Productivity aggressiveness and supervisory style', *Sociology and Social Research*, 65(2), pp.23-36.

Chusmir, L. H. and Koberg, C. S. (1988), 'Religion and attitudes towards work: A new look at an old question', *Journal of Occupational Behaviour*, 9, pp.251-262.

Clegg, S R (1992) 'Postmodern management?' *Journal of*

Organization Change Management, 5(2), pp.31-49.

Clegg, S. R. (1989), 'Radical revisions: power discipline and organizations', *Organization Studies*, 10(1), pp.97-115.

Clegg, C. W. and Wall, T. D. (1981), 'A note on some new scales for measuring aspects of psychological well being at work', *Journal of Occupational Psychology*, 54, pp.221-225.

Cobb, A. T. (1984), 'An episodic model of power: Toward an integration of theory and research', *Academy of Management Review*, 9(3), pp.482-93.

Cohen, E. A. (1953), *Human Endeavour in Concentration Camps*, Norton, New York.

Cook, J. D. and Wall, T. D. (1980), 'New work attitude measures of trust, organizational commitment and personal need non-fulfilment', *Journal of Occupational Psychology*, 53, pp.39-52.

Cook, J. D. Hepworth, S. J. Wall, T. D. and Warr, P. B. (1981), *The Experience of Work: A Compendium and Review of 249 Measures and Their Use*, Academic Press, London.

Crick, B. (1976), *In Defence of Politics*, Penguin, Harmondsworth.

Curry, J. P. Wakefield, D. S. Pierce, J. L. and Mueller, C. W. (1986), 'On the causal ordering of job satisfaction and organizational commitment', *Academy of Management Journal*, 29, pp.847-858.

Curry, L. 'Student commitment and school organization in relation to task behaviour and achievement', *Contemporary Education Psychology*, 9(2), pp.171- 184.

Curtis, R. L. Jr. (1989), 'Cutbacks, management, and human relations: meanings for organizational theory and research', *Human Relations*, 42(8), pp.671-689

Dahl, R. A. (1957), 'The concept of power', *Behavioral Science*, 2, pp.201-15.

Daily, R. L. (1986), 'Understanding organization commitment for volunteers - empirical and managerial implications', *Journal of Voluntary Action Research*, 15(1), pp.19-31.

Deming, E. (1986), *Out of the Crisis*, Cambridge, University Press, Cambridge.

203

Drummond, H. (1989), 'Power and Involvement in Organizations'. (Unpublished doctoral dissertation, University of Leeds, UK).

Drummond, H. (1990), *'Managing Difficult Staff'*, London, Kogan Page.

Drummond, H. (1991), *'Power'*, London, Kogan Page.

Drummond, H. (1992), 'Research note on the measurement of organization commitment', *The Management Development Journal of Singapore*, 3(1), pp.3- 11, (a).

Drummond, H. (1992), *'The Quality Movement'*, Kogan Page, London, (b).

Drummond, H. and Chell, E (1992) 'Should organizations pay for quality'? *Personnel Review*, 21(2), pp.3-11.

Dubin, R. (1956), 'Industrial workers worlds: A study of life interest of industrial workers', *Social Problems*, 13, pp.131-142.

Dubin, R. Champoux, J. E. and Porter, L. W. (1975), 'Central life interests and organizational commitment of blue collar and clerical workers', *Administrative Science Quarterly*, 20, pp.411-421.

Emerson, R. H. (1962), 'Power-dependence relations', *American Sociological Review*, 27, pp.31-41.

Etzioni, A. (1959), 'Authority structure and organizational effectiveness', *Administrative Science Quarterly*, 4, pp.43-47.

Etzioni, A. (1965), 'Dual leadership in complex organizations', *American Sociological Review*, 30, pp.688-698, (a).

Etzioni, A. (1965), 'Organizational control structure', In J. G. March (Ed.), *Handbook of Organizations*, Rand McNally, Chicago, (b).

Etzioni, A. 'Organizational dimensions and their inter-relationships: A theory of compliance', In B. P. Indik and K. Berrien (Eds.). (1968), *Peoples Groups and Organizations*, Teachers College Press, New York, (a).

Etzioni, A. (1968), *The Active Society*, Collier MacMillan, London, (b).

Etzioni, A. (1968), 'Basic human needs: Alienation and

inauthenticity', *American Sociological Review*, 33, pp.810-855, (c).

Etzioni, A. (1975), *A Comparative Analysis of Complex Organizations*, Collier MacMillan, London.

Etzioni, A., and Lehman, E.W. (1980), *A Sociological Reader on Complex Organizations*, Holt Reinhart and Winston, New York.

Farrell, D. and Rusbult, C. E. (1981), 'Exchange variables as predictors of job satisfaction, job commitment and turnover. The impact of rewards, costs, alternatives and investments', *Organizational Behaviour and Human Performance*, 27, pp.78-95.

Feidler, F. E. A (1967), *Theory of Leadership Effectiveness*. McGraw Hill, New York.

Fisher, R. and Ury, W. (1983), *Getting to Yes*, Hutchinson, London.

Fisher, C. D. (1980), 'On the dubious wisdom of expecting job satisfaction to correlate with organizational performance', *Academy of Management Review*, 4, pp.607-612.

Fourcher, L. A. (1975), 'Compliance structures and change within mental health service organizations', *Sociology of Work and Occupations*, 2(3), pp.246-256.

Franklin, J. L. (1975), 'Power and commitment - empirical assessment', *Human Relations*, 28(8), pp.737-753.

Freidson, E. (1984), 'The changing nature of professional control', *Annual Review of Sociology*, 10, pp.1-20.

French, J. R. and Raven, B. 'The bases of social power.' In D. Cartwright and A. Zander, (Eds.), (1968), *Group Dynamics*. Harper and Row, New York.

Gallagher, D. G. (1984), 'The relationship between organizational and union commitment among federal government employees', *Proceedings of the Academy of Management*, pp.319-323.

Galbraith, J. K. (1984), *The Anatomy of Power*, Hamish Hamilton, London.

Gaski, J. F. (1984), 'The theory of power and conflict in channels of distribution', *Journal of Marketing*, 48, pp.9-29.

Gerth, H. and Mills, C. W. In L. A. Coser, and B. Rosenberg (Eds.), (1982), *Sociological theory: A book of readings*, Collier MacMillan, New York.

Glaser, B. G. and Strauss, A. L. (1968), *The Discovery of Grounded Theory: Strategies for Qualitative Research*, Weidenfield and Nicholson, London.

Glaser, D. (1966), *The Effectiveness of a Prison Parole System*, Bobbs Merrill, New York.

Gorn, G. J. and Kanungo, R. N. (1980), 'Job involvement and motivation: Are intrinsically motivated managers more job involved'? *Organizational Behaviour and Human Performance*, 26, pp.265-277.

Gouldner, A. W. (1957), 'Cosmopolitans and locals: towards an analysis of latent social roles', *Administrative Science Quarterly*, 2, pp.281-306.

Greaves, C. (1948), *Women in Green*, Heineman, London.

Greene, C. N. and Podsakoff, P. M. (1981), 'Effects of withdrawal of performance contingent reward on supervisory influence and power', *Academy of Management Journal*, 24(3), pp.527-542.

Greene, C. N. (1972), 'Relationships among role accuracy, compliance, performance evaluation and satisfaction within managerial dyads', *Academy of Management Journal*. 15(2), pp.205-215.

Griffin, R. W. and Bateman, T. S. 'Job satisfaction and organizational commitment', In C. L. Cooper and I. Robertson (Eds.), (1986), *International Review of Industrial and Organizational Psychology*, John Wiley, New York.

Gross, E. and Etzioni, A. (1985), *Organizations in Society*, Prentice Hall, Engle Wood Cliffs.

Hackman, J. and Oldham, G. R. (1980), '*Work Redesign*', Reading, Addison-Wesley.

Hage, J. 'Theory building', In N. Nicholson and T. D. Wall (Eds.), (1982), *The Theory and Practice of Organizational Psychology*,

Academic Press, London.

Hall, D. T. Schneider, B. and Nygren, H. T. (1970), 'Personal factors in organizational identification', *Administrative Science Quarterly*, 15, pp.176-190.

Hall, R. H. Haas, J. E. and Johnson, N. J. (1967), 'An examination of the Blau-Scott and Etzioni typologies', *Administrative Science Quarterly*, 12, pp.118-139.

Handy, C. B. (1985), *Understanding Organizations*, 3rd Ed, Harmondsworth, Penguin.

Handy, C. B. (1990), *The Age of Unreason*, London, Arrow.

Heider, F. (1958), *The Psychology of Interpersonal Relations*, John Wiley, New York.

Hepburn, J. R. (1985), 'The exercise of power in coercive organizations - a study of prison guards', *Criminology*, 23(1), pp.145-164.

Hickson, D. J. Hinings, L. R. Lee, C. A. Schneck, R. E. and Pennings, J. M.(1971), 'A strategic contingencies theory of intra-organizational power', *Administrative Science Quarterly*, 16(2), pp.216-29.

Houghland, J. G. Shepard, J. M. and Wood, J. R. (1979), 'Discrepancies in perceived organizational control importance in local churches', *Sociological Quarterly*, 201, pp.63-76.

Houghland, J. G. and Wood, J. R. (1980), 'Control in church organizations and commitment of members', *Social Forces*, 39, pp.5-105.

Hrebiniak, L. G. and Alluto, J. A. (1972), 'Personal and role-related functions in the development of organizational commitments', *Administrative Science Quarterly*, 17, pp.555-573.

Hyman, J. M. (1977), 'Alienation and prisonization', *Criminology*, 15(2), pp.263-265.

Jackson, P. R. Stafford, C. M. Banks, M. H. and Warr, P. B. (1983), 'Unemployment and psychological distress in young people: The moderating role of employment commitment', *Journal of Applied Psychology*, 68(3), pp.525-535.

Jamal, M. (1974), 'Task specialization and organizational commitment: An empirical examination among blue collar workers', *Proceedings of the Academy of Management*, pp.236-250.

Johnson, R. D. (1973), *'An Investigation of the Interaction Effects of Ability*, and Motivational Properties in Task Performance. (Unpublished dissertation; Pudinna University').

Johnston, G. P. and Snizek, W. E. (1991), 'Combining head and heart in complex organizations: a test of Etzioni's dual compliance structure hypothesis', *Human Relations*, 44(12), pp.1255-1272.

Julian, J. (1966), 'Compliance patterns and communication blocks in complex organizations', *American Sociological Review*, 31, pp.382-389.

Julian, J. (1968), 'Organizational involvement and social control', *Social Forces*, 47, pp.12-16.

Kanter, R. M. (1968), 'Commitment and social organization. A study of commitment mechanisms in utopian communities', *American Sociological Review*, 33, pp.499-517.

Kanter, R. M. (1979), 'Power failure in management circuits', *Harvard Business Review*, June/July.

Kanungo, R. N. (1979), 'The concepts of alienation and involvement revisited', *Psychological Bulletin*, 36(1), pp.119-138.

Kanungo, R. N. (1982), *Work Alienation: An Integrative Approach*, Prager, New Y York.

Katz, D. Maccoby, N. and Morse, N. C. (1950), *Productivity, Supervision and Morale in an Office Situation*, Survey Research Centre, Ann Arbor University of Michigan.

Katz, D. (1964), 'The motivational basis of organizational behaviour', *Behavioral Science*, 9, pp.113-133.

Katz, F. W. (1982), 'Implementation of the holocaust, the behaviour of Nazi officials', *Comparative Study of Society*, 24 (3), pp.510-529.

Kaufman, W. (1970), 'The inevitability of alienation', In, R.

Schacht (Ed.), *Alienation,* Double Day, New York.

Kelman, H. C. (1958), 'Compliance, identification and internalization, three processes of attitude change', *Journal of Conflict Resolution,* 11(1), pp.51-60.

Kern, A. G. and Bahr, E. M. (1974), 'Some factors affecting leadership climate in a state parole agency', *Pacific Sociological Review,* 7(4), pp.108-118.

Kidron, A. (1978), 'Work values and organizational commitment', *Academy of Management Journal,* 21(2), pp.239-247.

Kieser, A. (1987), 'From asceticism to administration of wealth. Medieval monastries and the pitfalls of rationalization', *Organization Studies,* 8(2), pp.103-123.

Kieser, A. (1989), 'Organizational, institutional, and societal evolution: Medieval craft guilds and the genesis of formal organizations', *Administrative Science Quarterly,* 34, pp.540-564.

Kipnis, D. (1972), 'Does power corrupt?' *Journal of Personality and Social Psychology,* 24, pp.33-41.

Kipnis, D. (1976), *The Powerholders,* University of Chicago Press, Chicago.

Kipnis, D. Schmidit, S. M. Wilkinson, I. (1980), 'Intraorganizational influence tactics: Explorations in getting one's way', *Journal of Applied Psychology,* 65 (4), pp.440-452.

Knights, D. and Roberts, J. (1982), 'The power of organization and the organization of power', *Organization Studies,* 3(1), pp.47-63.

Korman, A. L, Glickman, A. S. and Frey, R. L. (1981) 'More is not better: two failures of incentive theory', *Journal of Applied Psychology,* 66(2), pp.255-259.

Kushman, J. W. (1992), 'The organizational dynamics of teacher workplace commitment: A study of urban elementary and middle schools'. *Educational Administration Quarterly,* 28(1), pp.5-42.

Kuhn, T. S. (1970), *The Structure of Scientific Revolutions,* Chicago, University of Chicago Press.

Lammers, C. J. (1988), 'The interorganizational control of an occupied country', *Administrative Science Quarterly*, 33, pp.438-457.

Larson, J. H. (1983), 'Rural female delinquents adaptation to institutional life', *Juvenile and Family Court Journal*, 34(1), pp.83-92.

Larson, J. H. and Nelson, J. (1984), 'Women, 'friendship and adaptation to prison', *Journal of Criminal Justice*, 12, pp.601-615.

Lawler, E. E. III. and Hall, D. T. (1970), 'Relationship of job characteristics to job involvement, satisfaction and intrinsic motivation', *Journal of Applied Psychology*, 54, pp.305-312.

Lawler, E. E. III. 'Challenging traditional research assumptions', In E. E. Lawler. A. M. Mohrman, Jr. S. A. Mohrman., G. E. Ledford, Jr. T. G. Cummings and Associates (Eds.), (1985), *Doing Research That Is Both Useful, For Theory And Practice*. Jossey-Bass, San Fransisco.

Lee, T. W. and Mitchell, T. R. (1991), 'The unfolding effects of organizational commitment and anticipated job satisfaction on voluntary employee turnover', *Motivation and Emotion*, 15(1), pp.99-121.

Lee, T. W. and Johnson, D. R. (1991), 'The effects of work schedule and employment status on the organizational commitment and job satisfaction of full versus part-time employees', *Journal of Vocational Behavior*, 38(2), pp.208-224.

Lee, T. W. and Mitchell, T. R. (1991), 'The unfolding effects of organizational commitment and anticipated job satisfaction on voluntary employee turnover', *Motivation and Emotion*, 15(1), pp.99-121.

Littler C. R. and Salaman, G. (1982), 'Bavermania and beyond: recent theories of the labour process', *Sociology*, 16, pp.251-263.

Luthans, F. and Kreitner, R. (1985), *'Organizational Behavior Modification and Beyond'*, (2nd ed). Glenview, Ill: Scott, Foresman and Co.

Leftkowitz, J. and Brigando, L. (1980), 'The redundancy of alienation and job satisfaction: Some evidence of convergent and discriminant validity', *Journal of Vocational Behaviour*, 16(2), pp.115-131.

Leftkowitz, J. Somers, J. M. and Weinberg, K. (1984), 'The role of need level and or need salience as moderators of the relationship between need satisfaction and work alienation and involvement', *Journal of Vocational Behaviour*, 24(2), pp.142-158.

Lehman, E. (1969), 'Toward a macrosociology of power', *American Sociological Review*, 34(4), pp.453-465.

Leplat, J. (1990), 'Skills and tacit skills: A psychological perspective', *Applied Psychology: An International Review*, 39, pp.143-151.

Levinson, D. J. (1978), *The Seasons of a Man's Life*, Knopf, New York.

Levinson, H. (1973), 'Asinine attitudes toward motivation', *Harvard Business Review*, 51, pp.76-77.

Likert, R. (1958), 'Measuring organizational performance', *Harvard Business Review*, 36, pp.41-50.

Lodahal, T. M. and Kejner, M. (1965), 'The definition and measurement of job involvement', *Journal of Applied Psychology*, 49, pp.24-33.

Losch, R. F. (1976), 'Sources of power: Their impact on intrachannel conflict', *Journal of Marketing Research*, 13, pp.382-90.

Lukes, S. (1974), *Power: A Radical View*, Macmillan, London.

Luthans, E. McCaul, H. S. and Dodd, N. G. (1985), 'Organizational commitment: A comparison of American, Japanese and Korean employees', *Academy of Management Journal*, 23(1), pp.213 - 219.

Makin, P. and Robertson, I. (1986), 'Selecting the best selection techniques', *Personnel Management*, November, pp.262-266.

Mann, F. and Dent, J. (1954), *Appraisals Of Supervisors*, University of Michigin', Ann Arbor Survey Research Centre.

Marsh, R. M. and Mannari, H. (1977), 'Organizational commitment and turnover: A prediction study', *Administrative Science Quarterly*, 12, pp.57-75.

Martin, J. C. (1981), 'Dual allegiance in public sector unionism. A case study', *International Review of Applied Psychology*, 30, pp.245-259.

Martin, R. (1977), *The Sociology of Power*, Routledge and Kegan Paul, London.

Maslow, A. H. (1954), *Motivation And Personality*, New York, Harper and Brother.

Mathieu, J. E. and Farr, J. L. (1991), 'Further evidence for the disciminant validity of measures of organizational commitment, job involvement and job satisfaction', *Journal of Applied Psychology*, 76(1), pp.127-133.

Mathieu, J. E. (1991), 'A cross-level nonrecursive model of the antecedents of organizational commitment and satisfaction', *Journal of Applied Psychology*, 76(5), pp.607-618.

Mathieu, J. E. and Zajac, D. M. (1990), 'A review and meta-analysis of the organizational commitment',

Mayer, R. C. and Schoorman, F. D. (1992), 'Predicting participation and production outcomes through a two-dimensional model of organization commitment', *Academy of Management Journal*, 35(3), pp.671-684.

McClelland, D. C. (1975), *Power: The Inner Experience*. Irvington, New York.

McGregor, D. (1960), *The Human Side Of Enterprise*, McGraw Hill, New York.

Mechanic, D. (1962), 'Sources of power of lower participants in complex organizations', *Administrative Science Quarterly*, 7(3), pp.349-364.

Meyer, J. P. Paunonen, S. V. Gellatly, I. R. Goffin, R. D. and Jackson, D. N. (1989), 'Organizational commitment and job performance: Its the nature of the commitment that counts', *Journal of Applied Psychology*, 74, pp.152-156.

Miller, G. Boster, F. Rolloff, M. and Siebold, D. (1977) 'Compliance gaining message strategies, typology and some findings concerning the effects of situational differences', *Communication Monographs*, 44(1), pp.37-51.

Miller, G. A. (1967), 'Professionals in bureaucracy: alienation among industrial scientists and engineers', *American Sociological Review*, 32, pp.755-768.

Mintzberg, H. (1979), *The Structuring of Organization: A Synthesis of the Research*, Prentice-Hall, Englewood Cliffs.

Mintzberg, H. (1983), *Power in and Around Organizations*, Prentice-Hall, Englewood Cliffs.

Mintzberg, H. (1984), 'Power and organizational life cycles', *Academy of Management Review*, 9(2), pp.207-224.

Mintzberg, H. (1983), *'Power in and Around Organizations'*. Englewood Cliffs, New Jersey.

Mitroff, I. I. 'Why our old pictures of the world do not work anymore', In E. E. Lawler, M. Mohrman, S. A. Mohrman, G. E. Ledford and T. G. Cummings, *(1985), Doing Research that is Useful for Theory and Practice*. Jossey Bass, London.

Morgan, G. (1986), *Images of Organization*, Sage, London.

Moore, T. and Wood, D. (1979), 'Power and the hospital executive', *Hospital and Health Services Administration*, 24, pp.30-41.

Morrow, P. L. (1983), 'Concept redundancy in organizational research: The case of work commitment', *Academy of Management Review*, 8(3), pp.486-500.

Morrow, P. L. and Melroy, J. C. (1986), 'On assessing measures of work commitment', *Journal of Occupational Behavior*, 7(2), pp.139-145.

Mowday, R. T. 'Equity theory predictions of behaviour in organizations', In R. W. Steers and L. W. Porter (Eds.), (1979), *Motivation and Work Behaviour* 2nd edn, Tokyo: McGraw-Hill.

Mowday, R. T. Steers, R. M. and Porter, L. W. (1979), 'The measurement of organizational commitment', *Journal of Vocational Behaviour*, 14, pp.224-247.

Mowday, R. T. Porter, L. and Steers, R. H. (1982), *Employee -*

Organization Linkages, The Psychology of Commitment, Absenteeism and Turnover, Academic Press, London.

Mulford, C. L. (1978), 'Why they don't even whey they ought to - implications of compliance theory for policy makers', *International Journal of Comparative Sociology*, 19, (1-2), pp.47-62.

Murphy, W. P. (1980), 'Secret knowledge as property and power in Kpelle Society - elders versus youth', *Africa*, 50 (2), pp.193-207.

Near, J. P. (1989), 'Organizational commitment among Japanese and U. S. workers', *Organization Studies*, 10(3), pp.281-300.

Nault, R. (1975), 'Voluntary and involuntary student participation in non public school settings - consequences for students and schools', *Notre Dame Journal of Education*, 6(4), pp.311-322.

Ng, S. H. (1980), *The Social Psychology of Power*, Academic Press, London.

Oliver, N. (1989), 'Coordination and control in a small producer cooperative: dynamics and dilemmas', *Economic and Industrial Democracy*, 10, pp.447-465.

Oliver, N. (1990), 'Rewards, investments, alternatives and organizational commitment: empirical evidence and theoretical development', *Journal of Occupational Psychology*, 63, pp.19-31.

O'Reilly III C. A. and Puffer, S. M. (1989), 'The impact of rewards and punishments in a social context: a laboratory and field experiment', *Journal of Occupational Psychology*, 62, pp.41-53.

Ornstein, S. (1986), 'Organizational symbols: A study of their meanings and influences on perceived organizational climates', *Organizational Behaviour and Human Decision Processes*. 38, pp.207- 229.

Parsons, T. (1960), *Structure and Process in Modern Societies*, Free Press of Glencoe, Illinois.

Patchen, M. (1970), *Participation, Achievement and Involvement on the Job*, Prentice Hall, New York.

Pearce, J. L. (1983), 'Comparing volunteers and employees in a test of Etzioni Compliance Typology', *Journal of Voluntary Action Research,* 12(2), pp.22-30.

Penley, L. E. and Gould, S. (1988), 'Etzioni's model of organizational involvement: A perspective for understanding commitment in organizations', *Journal of Organizational Behavior,* 9, pp.43-59.

Perrow, C. (1972), *Complex Organizations: A Critical Essay,* Scott Foresman and Co, Glenview Ill.

Pettigrew, A. (1973), *The Politics of Organizational Decision Making,* Tavistock, London.

Pfeffer, J. (1981), *Power in Organizations,* Pitman, Marshfield Mass.

Pfeffer, J. (1992), 'Understanding power in organizations', *California Management Review,* Winter, pp.29-50.

Podsakoff, P. M. (1982), 'Determinants of supervisors use of reward and punishment. A literature review and suggestions for future research', *Organizational Behavior and Human Performance,* 29, pp.58-83.

Podsakoff, P. M. Todor, W. D. and Skov, R. (1982), 'Effects of leader contingent and non-contingent reward and punishment behaviour on subordinate performance and satisfaction', *Academy of Management Journal,* 25(4), pp.810-821.

Podsakoff, P. M. Todor, W. D. Grover, B. A. and Huber, O. L. (1984), 'Situational moderators of leader reward and punishment behavior - fact or fiction', *Organization Behavior and Human Performance,* 34, pp.21-63.

Podsakoff, P. M. and Schreishcheim, C. A. (1985), 'Field studies of french and Raven's bases of social power: Critique reanalysis and suggestions for future research', *Psychological Bulletien,* 97(3), pp.387-411.

Podsakoff, P. M. and Todor, W. D. (1985), 'Relationships between leader reward and punishment behavior and group processes and productivity', *Journal of Management,* 11(1), pp.55-75.

Porter, L. W. and Smith, F. J. (1970), 'The Etiology of

Organizational Commitment', Unpublished paper', University of California, Irvine.

Porter, L. W. Steers, R. M. Mowday, R. T, and Boulian, P. V. (1974), 'Organizational commitment, job satisfaction, and turnover among psychiatric technicians', *Journal of Applied Psychology*, 59, pp.603-609.

Popper, M. and Lipshitz, R. (1992), 'Ask not what your country can do for you: the normative basis of organizational commitment', *Journal of Vocational Behavior*, 41, pp.1-12.

Price, J. L. and Meuller, C. W. (1981), 'A casual model of turnover for nurses', *Academy of Management Journal*, 24, pp.543-565.

Rabinowitz, S. and Hall, D. T. (1977), 'Organizational research on job involvement', *Psychological Bulletin* 84(2), pp.265-288.

Rahim, M. A. (1989), 'Relationships of leader power to compliance and satisfaction with supervision: evidence from a national sample of managers', *Journal of Management*, 15(4), pp.545-556.

Rahim, M. A. and Buntman, G. F. (1989), 'Supervisory power bases, styles of handling conflict with subordinates, and subordinate compliance and satisfaction', *The Journal of Psychology*, 123(2), pp.195-210.

Randall, D. M. (1987), 'Commitment and the organization: the organization man revisited', *Academy of Management Review*, 12(3), pp.460-471.

Randall, D. M. (1990), 'The consequences of organizational commitment', *Journal of Vocational Behavior*, 11(5), pp.361-378.

Randall, D. M. Fedor, D. B. and Longenecker, C. O. (1990), 'The behavioral expression of organizational commitment', *Journal of Vocational Behavior*, 36(2), pp.210-224.

Ray, C. A. (1986), 'Corporate culture: The last frontier of control', *Journal of Management Studies*, 23(3), pp.287-299.

Rothschild-Whitt, J. (1979), 'The collectivist organization: An alternative to rational bureacratic models', 44, pp.509-527.

Raven, B. H. and Kruglanski, A. E. (1970), 'Conflict and power', In P. Swingle (Ed.), *The Structure of Conflict.* New York, Academic Press.

Reichers, A. E. (1985), 'A review and reconceptualisation of organizational commitment', *Academy of Management Review,* 10(3), pp.465-476.

Reitz, H. J. (1971), 'Managerial attitudes and perceived contingencies between performance and organizational response', *Academy of Management Proceedings,* 21st Annual Meeting pp.227-238.

Robbins, S. P. (1983), *Organization Behavior: Concepts Controvesies and Applications,* Prentice Hall, Englewood Cliffs.

Roscoe, J. T. (1975), *Fundamental Research Statistics for the Behavioural Sciences,* Holt, Reinhart and Winston, New York.

Rose, M. (1975), *Industrial Behaviour: Theoretical Developments Since Taylor,* Allen Lane, London.

Rosen, B. and Jerdee, T. H. (1974), 'Factors influencing disciplinary judgements', *Journal of Applied Psychology,* 59, pp.327-331.

Rossel, R. (1970), 'Instrumental and expressive leadership in complex organizations', *Administrative Science Quarterly,* 15, pp.306-316.

Rossel, R. (1971), 'Required labor commitment, organizational adaptation, and leadership orientation', *Administrative Science Quarterly,* 16, pp.316-320.

Rouseau, D. M. (1977), 'Sociological differences in job characteristics, employee satisfaction and motivation: A synthesis of job design research and sociological and systems theory', *Organization Behavior and Human Performance.* 19, pp.18- 42.

Rusbult, C. E. (1980), 'Satisfaction and commitment in friendships', *Representative Research and Social Psychology,* 11, pp.78-95.

Rusbult, C. E. (1980), 'Commitment and satisfaction in romantic associations: A test of the investment model', *Journal of*

Experimental and Social Psychology, 16, pp.172-186.

Russel, B. (1938), Power: *A New Social Analysis,* George, Allen and Unwin, London.

Salancik, G. R. (1977), 'Commitment and the control of organizational behavior and belief', In B. M. Staw and G. R. Salancik (Eds.), *New Directions in Organizational Behaviour,* St Clair, Chicago.

Schnake, M. E. and Dumler, M. P. (1989), 'Some unconventional thoughts on the use of punishments in organizations: Reward as punishment and punishment as reward', *Journal of Social Behavior and Personality,* 4(1), pp.97-107.

Schriescheim, C. A. Hinkin, T. R. and Tetrault, L. A. (1991), 'The discriminant validity of the Leader Reward and Punishment Questionnaire (LRPQ) and satisfaction with supervision: A two sample, factor analytic investigation', *Journal of Occupational Psychology,* 64, pp.159-166.

Schein, E. H. (1980), *Organizational Psychology* (3rd Ed.), Prentice Hall, Englewood Cliffs.

Schneider, B. (1985), 'Organizational behaviour', *In Annual Review of Psychology,* 36, pp.573-611.

Seeman, M. (1959), 'On the meaning of alienation', *American Sociological Review,* 24, pp.783-791.

Senter, R. Miller, R. Reynolds, L. T. and Schaffer, T. (1983), 'Bureaucratization and goal succession in alternative organizatons', *Sociological Forces,* 16(4), pp.239-253.

Shaw, B. M. (1981), 'The escalation of commitment to a course of action', *Academy of Management Review,* 6(4), pp.557-587.

Shepard, J. M. (1971), *Autonomy and Alienation: A Study of Office and Factory Workers,* MIT Press, Mass.

Silverman, D. (1970), *The Theory of Organizations,* Heineman, London.

Simmel, G. (1950), *The Sociology of George Simmel,* Tr by K. H. Wolff, The Free Press, Glencoe Ill.

Simon, H. A. (1957), *Administrative Behavior* (2nd Ed.), Free Press, New York.

Sims, H. P. and Szilagyi, A. D. (1975), 'Leader reward behaviour and satisfaction and performance', *Organizational Behavior and Human Performance*, 14, pp.426-438.

Sims, H. P., Jr. (1980), 'Further thought on punishment in organizations', *Academy of Management Review*, 5(1), pp.133-138.

Sims, H. P. Jr. and Manz, C. C. (1984), 'Observing leader verbal behavior - toward reciprocal determinism in leadership theory', *Journal of Applied Psychology*, 69(2), pp.222-232.

Stevens, J. M. Beyer, J. M. and Trice, H. M. (1978), 'Assessing personal, role and organizational predictors of organizational commitment', *Academy of Management Journal*, 21, pp.380-396.

Smith, C. A. Organ, D. and Near, J. (1983), 'Organizational citizenship behavior: Its nature and antecedents', *Journal of Applied Psychology*, 68, pp.653-663.

Smith, C. G. W. and Hepburn, J. R. (1979), 'Alienation and prison organizations - comparative analysis', *Criminology*, 17(2), pp.251-262.

Speckman, R. E. (1979), 'Influence and information, an exploratory investigation of the boundary role person's basis of power', *Academy of Management Journal*, 22(1), pp.104-117.

Steers, R. M. (1977), 'Antecedents and outcomes of organizational commitment', *Administrative Science Quarterly*, 22, pp.46-56.

Stepina, L. P. Perrewe, P. L. Hassell, B. L. Harris, J. R. and Mayfield, C. R. (1991), 'A comparative test of the independent effects of inter-personal, task and reward domains on personal and organizational outcomes', *Journal of Social Behavior and Personality*, 6(1), pp.93-104.

Sterba, R. L. A. (1978), 'Clandestine management in imperial Chinese bureaucracy', *Academy of Management Review*, pp.69-78.

Stephenson, T. (1985), *Management: A Political Activity*, MacMillan, London.

Stojkovik, S. (1986), 'Social bases of power and control

mechanisms among correctional administrators in a prison organization', *Journal of Criminal Justice*, 14(2), pp.157-166.

Thomas, C. W. (1975), 'Theoretical perspectives on alienation in the prison society: An empirical test', *Pacific Social Review*, 18, pp.483-499.

Thomas, C. W. and Poole, C. D. (1975), 'The consequences of incompatible goal structures in correlational settings', *International Journal of Criminology and Penology*. 3, pp.27-42.

Thomas, C. W. Kreps, G. A. and Cage, R. (1977), 'Application of compliance theory to study of juvenile delinquency', *Sociology and Social Research*, 61(2), pp.156-175.

Thomas, C. W. Peterson, D. M. Zingraff, R. M. (1978), 'Structural and social psychological correlates of prisonization', *Criminology*, 16(3), pp.383-393.

Thomas, C. W. and Zingraff, M. T. (1976), 'Organizational structure as a determinant of prisonization - an analysis of the consequences of alienation', *Pacific Sociological Review*, 19(1), pp.96-116.

Tjosvold, D. (1985), 'The effects of attribution and social context on superior's influence and interaction with low performing subordinates', *Personnel Psychology*, 38(2), pp.361-376, (a).

Tjosvold, D. (1985), 'Power and social context in superior subordinate interaction', *Organizational Behaviour and Human Decision Processes*. 35(3), pp.281-293, (b).

Torres, C. McIntosh, W. A. and Zey, M. (1991), 'The effects of bureaucratization and commitment on resource mobilization in voluntary organizations', *Sociological Spectrum*, 11, pp.19-44.

Trice, H. P. and Beyer, J. M. (1977), 'Differential use of alchoholism policy in federal organizations between different levels of employees', In C. J. Schramm (Ed.), *Employee Assistance and Alcoholism Programs in American Industry*, John Hopkins Press, Baltimore.

Trist, E. L. and Bamforth, K. W. (1951), 'Some sociological and psychological consequences of the long-wall method of coal-getting', *Human Relations*, 4, pp.3-38.

Vandenberg, R. J. and Lance, C. E. (1992), 'Examining the causal order of job satisfaction and organizational commitment', *Journal of Management*, 18(1), pp.153-167.

Vancouver, J. B. and Schmidt, N. W. (1991), 'An exploratory examination of person-organization fit: organizational goal congruence', *Personnel Psychology*, 44(2), pp.333-352.

Vechio, R. P. and Sussmann, M. (1989), 'Preferences for forms of supervisory influence', *Journal of Organizational Behavior*, 10, pp.135-143.

Vroom, K. H. (1962), 'Ego involvement, job satisfaction and job performance', *Personnel Psychology*, 15, pp.159-177.

Wall, T. D. and Lischeron, J. A. (1977), *Worker Participation: A Critique of the Literature and Some Fresh Evidence*. McGraw-Hill, Maidenhead.

Wall. T. D. Kemp, N. J. Jackson, P. R. and Clegg, C. W. (1986), 'Outcome of autonomous work groups: A long term field experiment', *Academy of Management Journal*, 29(2), pp.280-304.

Warr, P. Cook, J. and Wall, T. D. (1979), 'Scales for the measurement of some work attitudes and aspects of psychological well being', *Journal of Occupational Psychology*, 52, pp.129-148.

Warren, D. I. (1968), 'Power, visbility and conformity in formal organizations', *American Sociological Review*, 33(6), pp.951-70.

Witt, L. A. and Beorkem, M. N. (1991), 'Satisfaction with initial work assignment and organizational commitment', *Journal of Applied Social Psychology*, 21(21), pp.1873-1792.

Winfree, L. T. and Wolfe, L. M. (1980), 'Sources of rebellion in two institutions for juvenile offenders', *Juvenile and Family Court Journal*, 31(1), pp.51-70.

Wood, J. R. (1975), 'Legitimate control and organizational transendance', *Social Forces*. 54(1), pp.199-211.

Wood, S. (1990), 'Tacit skills, the Japanese management model and new technology', *Applied Psychology: An International Review*, 39, pp.169-190.

Wrong, D. H. (1979), *Power, Its Forms Bases and Uses*. Basil Blackwell, Oxford.

Zahn, G. L. Wolf, G. (1981), 'Leadership and the art of cycle maintenance: A stimluation model of superior subordinate interaction', *Organization Behavior and Human Performance*, 28 (1), pp.26-49.